MW01166592

Finding My Way Home

Fighting Depression
Backpacking in Central Florida

BY ROB ROGERS

All rights reserved. No part of this publication may be reproduced in whole or in part, or stored in a retrieval system, or transmitted in any form or by any means, electronic, mechanical, photocopying, recording, or otherwise, without written permission of the author, except for the inclusion of brief quotations in a review.

Copyright © 2024 by Rob Rogers

For information regarding permission, please write to:
info@barringerpublishing.com
Barringer Publishing, Naples, Florida
www.barringerpublishing.com

Cover, graphics, and layout by Linda S. Duider
Cape Coral, Florida

ISBN: 978-1-954396-77-7
Library of Congress Cataloging-in-Publication Data
Finding My Way Home: Fighting Depression Backpacking in Central Florida / Rob Rogers

Printed in U.S.A.

*To Kelly, Kara, and Claire, and
not necessarily in that order.*

TABLE OF CONTENTS

Flooded portions of Florida National Scenic Trail at the Osceola National Forest, April 9, 2024.

CHAPTER ONE

Alone on the Trail

I knew I was in trouble when the chilly water rose above my ankles and I could no longer see the trail.

I was on, or rather near, the Florida National Scenic Trail, returning from an out-and-back one-nighter in the Osceola National Forest, on a stretch known by experienced backpackers to be wet, but I had attempted to find the wrong way past the wettest part. I had crossed this stretch the day before on a boardwalk, but its northern end had washed out halfway through and I needed to bushwhack through a dense thicket of palmetto and thorny vines beside the rest of this submerged stretch of trail. I had to bushwhack again at the beginning of the same stretch this morning, but I picked the wrong side of the trail, and now it was too late to turn back.

Before even leaving this part of the trail, I had already fallen twice when thorny vines tied my legs, and I soon again felt the stinging and tearing of more needly thorns as I panted again through the brush. My stomach began to wretch as I realized the predicament in which I had become entangled. To get through this stretch quickly, I had gone too far too fast to see a way back, and the water was getting deeper.

1

I struggled in vain to find higher ground to peer over the morass of jungle and black water to look for an open section that looked like the trail. I finally found a fallen tree, but its bark melted off like the candy coating of an overheated M&M when I stepped on it, and I fell into the swamp backpack-first. The icy chill of swamp water on my waist and chest froze my nerves as panic began to creep in. I finally managed to balance myself by using a branch as a wobbly cane, but I could see nothing but swamp in every direction. My spongy glob of a map was worthless. I sighed as I attempted to open my soaked cell phone with my cold, wet fingers to no avail. I suppressed the urge to childishly whimper a cry for help to a forest of cypress that would not answer.

It was at this moment that I thought, *I'm glad I took my Prozac this morning.*

Five months earlier, I could not have imagined sleeping in a tent, much less lugging more than 30 pounds to and from a backcountry campsite. But I had come a long way since then.

So I took a deep breath, patted myself on the back for getting this far, and started wading in the general direction of the trail. I used my walking stick to swat away the thorny vines, and as the water rose above my waist, I remembered noticing the day before that the water had run toward the boardwalk. I therefore followed the current, hoping the water was too cold for snakes. After I rounded a dense patch of trees, the boardwalk appeared on the far side of a black stream that was technically the Florida Trail. I muttered a pitiful "Yes!" as my terror quickly turned to relief.

The water was too deep to cross, so I slogged with pulsing legs parallel to the boardwalk back to where it began, crossed the stream, climbed onto the boardwalk, and dried off my electronics. The phone eventually sprang back to life; the nicotine vape was now a snorkel. As the swamp water cooled my adrenaline-fueled sweat, I told myself that I'm now a real backpacker.

I then continued down the five remaining miles of trail to my car, with a big shit-eating grin on my face the whole way.

I love longleaf pine trees.

I enjoy laying atop a picnic table or bench at a backcountry campsite after a long hike, covered in sweat, panting with exhaustion, and staring up long branchless trunks, until you reach the canopy at its apex where a pyramid of crispy boughs covered in pine needles stands like a summer Christmas tree. I walk beneath them on the trail and search for pinecones, using their size to determine whether they are longleaf, loblolly, or scrub pine. I laugh at myself when I try in vain to throw the rope for my bear bag to one of their lower limbs and test my patience for twenty minutes, hoping that the weighted end will finally catch a limb and fall within grasping distance, so I can stop swearing and sweating in frustration. I admire newly grown pines where the Christmas trees that eventually rise above the rest of the forest have already bloomed and will remain with the trees as they grow; my wife calls them *pom-pom pines*. It's thrilling to see some with thick trunks and wondering how many souls still alive today were around when

Live oaks at Myakka River State Park, February 23, 2024

their pom-poms first sprouted from the sandy forest floor. And I especially note when they grow from the middle of live oaks and are split by lightning, wind, or the ravages of time.

I also love live oaks. I revere their huge trunks that part near the ground and their limbs and branches that grow in every direction, like animated characters from a Tolkien fantasy. I love thinking about how British sailors ventured deep into Florida's forests before Thomas Jefferson wrote the *Declaration of Independence*, to seek out their massive V-shaped trunks that were better for building curved parts of their ships than arrow-straight planks. I relish how bromeliads, pink lichens, and especially blankets of moss cling to their branches and hang over the trails I hike and perfectly frame the rays of the rising sun. And the birds that nest in their canopies and begin singing as those rays of morning sunshine begin bathing their nests. I especially cherish sleeping beneath their boughs on a rainless night with the rain cover of my tent rolled back, staring at the stars and an occasional meteor through their protective arms. You have never lived until you have slept beneath a live oak.

I love the birds that fly among the pine and live oaks. The startled hawks that often greet me on the trail by swooping down from a nearby branch, passing mere feet over my head to perch on a branch further down the trail, seeming to stare at me with disdain for the disruption. I enjoy my embarrassment when I ignore a vulture perched atop a pine tree near my campsite (vultures are ubiquitous in Florida), only to realize that the ugly scavenger is actually a beautiful bald eagle. I venerate the ospreys and the nests they build atop dead pine trees and discovering those nests by seeing the

Reclining atop the wobbly picnic table at PCZ East campsite, at the Croom Tract of the Withlacoochee State Forest, February 28, 2024.

telltale droppings and feathers at the base of dead trees I pass on the trail. And I cherish the owls—I rarely see them, but I always hear them calling to each other through the forest in the early morning before dawn, first four hoots, then an answer with three hoots, and I'm occasionally lucky enough to listen to them all night long.

I admire the mammals I see on the trail. I prize the white tail deer that I see all over Central Florida that are easy to find at sunset and sunrise in open forest, especially the ones who frequent heavily toured state parks and therefore do not even twitch when you surprise them on the trail. I love the wild hogs, those temperamental snorting vacuum cleaners that raise the heart rates of informed hikers who find them binging on the trail with young who they defend aggressively. I treasure those few black bears I have been lucky enough to see away from state park dumpsters, with their you-can't-scare-me ambivalence and dark black eyes and fur. I adore the wild horses that freely roam Paynes Prairie and the cows that moo through the night near Lake Kissimmee State Park, just to let me know that I'm only so far from civilization. And I am amused at the armadillos and opossums that startle me on the trail or attempt to rummage through the firewood I leave lying on the ground, even when they ignore my firm instructions to go away while I pound my walking stick on a nearby tree, although I don't particularly enjoy them rattling through palmettos less than 10 feet from my tent while I'm trying to sleep.

I even enjoy the scaly reptiles for which Florida is famous, although it's more fearful respect and admiration. I endure the mild strokes I suffer when surprised by black racers darting across the trail inches from my boots on morning hikes, or the substantially more severe strokes I suffer when I see a copperhead or an eastern diamondback along the trail. And I even like the alligators I see during the summer in swamps and on the banks of creeks and spring-fed rivers (after all, I did spend my formative years at the University of Florida), with their opaque shot glass sized teeth, remorseless stares, thick body armor, and presumably also a few household pets in their bellies. But I hope I never see one again beside me on the trail.

I especially treasure sunrises and sunsets. Growing up in Florida, I've appreciated them for a long time, and certainly became more enamored with them while visiting my wife's parents' bayside home in North Redington Beach for decades before I began solo backpacking. For years, I've stayed at old school hotels in St. Pete Beach, watching the sun melt into the Gulf of Mexico after dinner and the sky changing color like a Turner painting as the last rays fall beneath the western horizon (I call that the *suffering*). I really came to appreciate sunsets and sunrises after my wife put a pool and patio into our backyard with my ambivalent approval, after which I began reading for an hour each morning before beginning my workday. Especially when depression and anxiety returned, I found comfort watching the sun setting over my neighbors' roofs.

But I had never truly experienced sunrises until I began awaiting their arrival while holding my full bladder in my coffin-sized tent beneath the live oaks. Or until I started eating freeze-dried backpacking dinners with a spork while watching the sun set behind ponds near backcountry campsites, and then watched the sun climb down the waterside pine trees the next morning, first inching slowly down the tree tops, then the trunks, then finally hitting the glassy water as cranes searched for breakfast.

And I adore the stars. The hundreds of stars that you can never see near theme parks or cities that whitewash the night sky. I love staring at Orion's belt in the winter and being able to see the rest of the archer with taut bow that I had never noticed before I slept in the forest alone. I love understanding what Brandon Boyd of Incubus meant when he wrote that the sky resembles a backlit canopy with holes punched in it. I enjoy tending a campfire and scaring away opossums without turning on a flashlight, seeing the furniture of my campsite illuminated by nothing but the stars and the moon gleaming down like a spotlight.

I am enchanted by everything about tending a campfire. With a restless mind that never takes a break, I love pacing non-stop around a fire ring, turning logs with my walking stick, and dodging kernels of burning pine bark as they explode softly while soaked with soft flames. I derive twisted pleasure in struggling to start a fire in 80 percent humidity and wondering why even the paper bag in which I carried kiln-dried kindling loses the flame seconds after I ignite it with my gas station lighter, before I can lower it to the embers fighting to survive the mist. I take delight in standing naked beside a fire, choking on smoke as I attempt to dry my dirty arms and legs and sweaty unmentionables with my sweaty socks, hoping the fire stays lit long enough to coat my body odor with smoke that just might deter mosquitoes and allow me to sleep in my tent. There is a wonderful sense of pride

I feel when I manage to keep a fire alive for three hours by teasing the damp dead pine branches and twigs to take over the job of sustaining the fire from the kiln-dried log and kindling that I carried into camp. Often, I do not notice how that fire has also consumed my endless negativity that often prevents me from falling asleep in my bed at home.

Of course, those are not the only things I love. I am thrilled by rock concerts and college football games, Las Vegas casinos, and watching drunk women flirt with strangers in pools at Las Vegas day clubs. I love playing aggressive, angry alternative rock music at 100 percent volume with distorted guitars that sound like bandsaws cutting through tooth enamel. I savor traveling to European cities and castles, art galleries, and other places far from starlit campfires, and visiting state history museums in American cities outside Florida. And reading books about history, geology, and art that are far too heavy to lug to a primitive campsite.

But few of those things give me the serenity and peace that I find on the trail, tending a campfire and sleeping beneath the stars, live oaks, and longleaf pines.

I had hiked for years in state and national parks before I began solo backpacking. My family hiked in the backcountry of Glacier National Park during a family reunion with my wife's siblings who lived in Idaho and Montana. My wife and daughter also got a kick out of watching me pant with exhaustion during a seven-mile loop hike with more than 1,000 feet of elevation gain that I had insisted we try in North

Cascades National Park. I needed the generosity of strangers and their electrolyte tablets during the descent, watching in exasperation as my daughter hopped up and down the mountain like one of the Super Mario brothers.

I would never have backpacked or slept in a tent back then. I weighed 275 pounds and had sleep apnea that caused snoring so loud that it could have triggered an avalanche. I had been overweight all my life, had weighed more than 235 pounds since shortly after my wedding in 2006, and was rarely able to lose more than 10 pounds at a time—even when "training" for annual pleasure weekends in Las Vegas.

That all changed in April of 2023. After becoming upset by a minor conflict with my wife, I continued to stew throughout the weekend after my wife and I made peace. By that Monday, I no longer had an appetite and went without any food all day Monday and Tuesday. But I continued to work from home, and after a stressful day at work on Tuesday while continuing to brood, I attempted to relieve that stress by walking three miles in my neighborhood.

I expected to feel better when I returned home. I did not. But I also expected my appetite to return, and I expected to eat a huge dinner to replace the food I had not eaten for the prior two days. I instead ate only a light meal, still bitter and brooding. The next morning, I stepped on the scale and had lost almost five pounds. I immediately realized that I may have an opportunity to finally lose a decent amount of weight, if I could continue exercising while reducing my diet by eating only a *normal person's* dinner and having only one dessert, rather than the three or four I typically ate each night before going to bed after midnight.

11

By that Friday, I had not yet gained back the weight and had dropped a few more pounds. I also continued to eat smaller breakfasts, lunches, reasonable dinners, and only one small dessert each night. I continued to have the energy to walk three miles after work that Wednesday and Friday. Although my stomach was screaming for chocolate and pizza, my mood had finally improved, and I began feeling that most precious of commodities—self-esteem. I also had a transatlantic flight coming in three months for a family vacation, so I had good reason to keep at it. If I could only lose 15 pounds, I might be able to avoid heartburn while being crammed into the tiny coach seat with 31-inch seat pitch for nine hours. I also knew the flight was going to be worse than ever if I didn't try something, as I had gained so much weight that I had endured my first experience two months earlier of being unable to fit into a roller coaster seat.

I reached my goal quickly—too quickly, I thought at the time. I realized that I could more comfortably walk on pavement while wearing Tevas with socks rather than walking shoes, so even though I looked like a fat dork with poor fashion sense, I was able to walk three miles three times a week. After two weeks of misery and withdrawal from a laundry list of foods I loved, I was continuing to shrink my stomach by reducing portion size. I also stopped eating breakfast, and reduced my lunch from two large sandwiches to a single smaller sandwich. I also continued to eat only one dessert a night but I replaced cookies and ice cream with dry whole grain cereal. As the days passed, I began craving that cereal and multigrain toast, and I no longer craved cookies, potato chips, or pizza. I reached my 15-pound weight loss goal more than a month and a half before our trip, and friends began noticing.

I was thrilled by my progress, which I had never made before. But I also knew that I had a month and a half to keep the weight off, and if I gained it back, I was not sure I could count on another two-day period without appetite to lose it again. My only choice was to double-down and continue eating less and walking three miles three times a week, even as evening temperatures and humidity rose as the Central Florida summer began.

It worked. By the time we left for our vacation, I was down 30 pounds and was gaining self-esteem, as well as compliments from kind neighbors. What's more, I had no reason to expect that the vacation would set me back. My wife and I do not believe in relaxing vacations, and my wife estimates that we walked more than 70 miles during our eight-day vacation, crisscrossing Amsterdam, Utrecht, Bruges, the Flanders Fields, and Brussels while fueling ourselves with Belgian chocolate, fresh fruit from street markets, and occasional ice cream cones. When I returned home, I was down another five pounds, and I was highly motivated to continue seeing how much weight I could lose.

From there, the weight loss reached exhilarating life-altering proportions. I was down almost 45 pounds by my birthday at the end of July and celebrated by reserving a cabana along the Wekiva River, where I relished keeping my shirt off all day among friends with whom I would never have dreamed of sharing my fat before. I increased my walking in the Central Florida heat of August to four miles four evenings a week, with predictable consequences to my mood, as I experienced more days of appetite suppressing negativity. But going days without eating did not undermine my weight loss, and as I continued to lose weight at an average of twelve pounds per month, my self-esteem and mood bounced back.

I then continued to lose weight even during football season, maintaining the pace through September and October and still losing five pounds in November. (The five weeks between Halloween and Thanksgiving are my holiday season—I never miss the Florida-Georgia game in Jacksonville, and the Florida State game is my Christmas even when I know my Gators will lose. So I did not restrain my beer consumption during that time.)

It was around this time that I started to realize I would be extremely upset if I gained back even half the weight I had lost, so I started considering activities for pleasure that would allow me to keep the weight off. I have never enjoyed working out at gyms, and although I appreciated the recent results of walking, I found it boring. I was also starting to notice that I spent my walks brooding about work, so I needed to find fun things to do that incorporate physical activity and keep me from the refrigerator.

For years, I had enjoyed hiking to train for vacations to national parks. I planned to resume hiking after football season, but I knew that wouldn't be enough. I therefore returned to hiking earlier than I had initially planned. Rather than drive to football games in Gainesville with friends and return the same night, I spent the night twice and hiked at nearby Paynes Prairie Preserve State Park. I also began hiking each weekend at Lake Louisa State Park near my home in Winter Garden, now known affectionately by my family as *LL*.

By the beginning of December, I was down to 205 pounds, and my wife began buying me new clothes because my current wardrobe was making me look like a fourth grader wearing his dad's suits. The sleep apnea that had tormented me for years was abating, and I was routinely able to sleep well on nights when I forgot to use my CPAP machine. It was only a matter of time before I remembered the two week-long backpacking trips I took as a Boy Scout and rediscovered backpacking. At almost the very moment that occurred, severe problems with depression and anxiety that I had last experienced decades earlier returned and knocked my world off its axis.

This is the story of my love affair with the outdoors near my home in Central Florida during nine one and two-night trips solo backpacking in the Florida wilderness from January 2024 through early April 2024, at the ripe old age of 47 years, after having not slept outdoors since adolescence. This is not really a story about mental illness, although my depression and anxiety are necessary for context. I also suspect that people suffering from depression or those who love them may find hope in my story and how my love affair with the Florida wilderness helped me cope with demons that have haunted me my whole life.

I would never pretend that I am a true outdoorsman. I carry far too much unnecessary gear and more than 20 percent of my weight, including an airport neck pillow, deodorizing body wipes for a "yuppie shower" before bed, kiln-dried kindling, and a kiln-dried log or two to cheat on fire in Florida's humidity. In all the nights I've now spent backpacking and on countless days I've spent hiking, I have yet to make a number two in the woods and even take Imodium to avoid the experience. And with a family and a busy career, I just cannot take off three months to follow a dream to thru hike, no matter how fulfilling that dream might be. Especially since I just took off three months to cope with depression.

But I do now consider myself a backpacker, even if only a beginner. I leave no trace of my presence at campsites other than the occasional unconsumed kiln-dried log. I sleep in a tent too small for anything other than my sleeping pad and sleeping bag, and I carry light titanium cookware and prepare meals on a camping stove the size of my thumb when it's folded. I keep my backpacking gear in a closet in my man cave and pack meticulously before trips. I rely on printed maps instead of cell phone apps (not that it helps keep me on my selected routes). I had done none of these less than five months before getting myself stuck in the swamp in the Osceola National Forest.

It's neither my intention to recommend that you retreat to the woods like Thoreau to avoid the evils of the world, nor to recommend that everyone suffering from depression or anxiety seek to cure their ails by solo backpacking. Several national parks sell books detailing the bad things that have happened to depressed people who searched for relief from pain in the backcountry, including bad things that many of those unfortunate people did to themselves.[1] I also did not write this book to advocate for the preservation of green spaces or threatened plants and animals, although I certainly support those who do.

I am writing this memoir of three transformative months of my life to share what I have learned and done because anyone can do it, even if they are middle aged like me, so long as they're in reasonably decent shape or are on the path toward it. Anyone can experience what I have experienced—for less than the cost of a standard vacation—if they just try. You do not have to hike the Appalachian Trail or climb a mountain. You can do what I've done in your own backyard, in natural spaces that you perhaps do not even know exist but drive by every day. Wonderful places that will make you feel more connected with and captivated by where you call home. These places might even make you enjoy more evenings in your backyard, watching the sunset, or sleeping with your bedroom curtains open just to watch the sun come up every morning. And they might just change your life.

Green Swamp, West Tract, June 3, 2024.

CHAPTER TWO

My Unquiet Mind[2]

𝒥n retrospect, it's not surprising that I planned and executed nine solo backpacking trips in three months without a blueprint.

A longtime season ticket holder for Florida Gators football, I've been planning road trips to UF road games for twenty years, studying maps and flight schedules for trips to every other SEC school. Since joining Florida Citrus Sports, the charity that hosts Orlando's two bowl games and allows its members to scout college football games at their own expense, I have also planned similar trips to Big Ten, Big 12, and ACC schools. For more than 15 years, I planned annual stress-relief weekends to Las Vegas after learning how to earn comps and receiving comped rooms during the subprime mortgage crisis. I scoured hotel booking websites, measured driving times from airports to hotels, and combed flight schedules to find the best direct flights.

In the ten years I worked at a big national law firm, I billed 2,000 hours a year and spent countless additional hours attending American Bar Association conferences and serving on the boards of directors of local charities, some of which recognized me with awards for my service. I was also writing five or more articles a year for legal publications and speaking at statewide and national legal conferences. I was also reading more than ten books a year. Aside from the lack of recognition I received from the law firm, I enjoyed all of it.

All of this is the product of having a restless mind that loves to learn, analyze, and plan. I have never been able to stop thinking, dreaming, and planning. My mind just can't manage boredom. I have never been able to just sit and rest. Even when at rest, my mind is always dreaming about and planning what's next. I am not trying to brag about these eccentricities or suggesting that you need to have them to solo backpack. These quirks just suggest why it was inevitable that I would plan and execute nine solo backpacking trips in three months once I got the urge to return to the forest.

These eccentricities made me somewhat of a weird, intense kid. In elementary school, I studied baseball cards and memorized statistics and lineups. I would spend hours all summer alone in my backyard playacting baseball games inning-by-inning and batter-by-batter, inserting myself into my favorite team's lineup at shortstop. In little league, my dad bought me a book describing where every fielder should move in every situation when balls were hit in play, and I applied those lessons in my games and later in life when playing recreational softball and kickball.

But these eccentricities were not without their drawbacks.

I have felt alone for most of my life, especially in crowded rooms and networking events. I have met few people throughout my life who share my interest in learning things that have no practical application. That is not to say that I think I'm smarter than everyone else. I have met many people who are much smarter than me. But I have met few people who share or admire my interest in reading books or learning just for the sake of learning, and I have met many people who think less of that most sacred part of who I am.

As you might expect, I've always had trouble making friends. When I'm comfortable with people, I have an intense personality that refuses to be politically correct and speaks the truth no matter how uncomfortable it makes them feel. I learned early in life that this does not make a good first impression, and I am therefore quiet and invisible in crowds. I have never understood why people think and act so differently than I do; I only know that they do. I also know from painful life experience that most people do not embrace nonconformity—especially the popular people who dictate what everyone else thinks. To harken back to early 1990s MTV, I have always felt like the bumblebee girl in Blind Melon's "No Rain" video who is ignored and misunderstood until she finds a colony of other bee people—except I have yet to find my bee people.

Even in early childhood, I could tell I was different. I always felt more emotional attachment to friends than they seemed to feel toward me. I was also unusually intense about anything I liked. When my sister and I started riding in a van to a private school near Pittsburgh and the driver played B-94 FM, I became infatuated with pop music and began writing my own Top 40 lists. I also became obsessed with song lyrics and movie lines and always related them to the events of my life. I decided immediately after my first little league game that I wanted to play baseball professionally, even after my father tactfully explained, "Most pro baseball players have special talent, and then there are a few like Pete Rose who get there just by hard work. You're going to have to be Pete Rose." I practiced relentlessly anyway.

But I suffered from no one seeming to notice me. I've come to realize recently that other people are not cold and uncaring, they just do not have the same intensity as me and have things on their mind other than me and my ambitions. But from the earliest age, I needed more attention than everyone else. Until recently, I never knew why.

I am not sure when I began being difficult for my family, but I know it was early in life. I was always too much trouble for my parents. I fought relentlessly with my younger sister, always bickering with her as most siblings do, but it seemed more frequent and more persistent. Nothing I did ever made me feel happy or fulfilled.

Going to a private school far from home did not help. My only friends lived across western Pennsylvania, so I never saw them outside of school except at my birthday party, and having a birthday in late July sucks because three months is a long time to wait to see your friends. I never exploited more local opportunities to make friends. I never socialized with my little league teammates off the field. While my sister spent weekends and summers playing with neighbors, I spent those days alone in my backyard immersed in fantasies and playacting sports and G.I. Joe patrols. And after we moved from western Pennsylvania on July 31, 1987—two days after my 11th birthday—I never spoke again with anyone we left behind in Pennsylvania other than a handful of family members.

The role of my parents in my early childhood is tricky to recall fairly. Because of the problems we had after we moved to Florida, I've never been able to give them the credit they deserve, but I know they were good parents early in my life for varied reasons.

My father has always been a kind and invested father. He coached every baseball team I ever played on and later remained an adult leader in my Boy Scout troop, even when his involvement exacerbated the growing divide between us. After every little league game, he bought fountain Cokes for every kid on the team. During my painful awakening to the cold-blooded competitiveness of youth sports in Florida after our move, he helped me cope with my tears in front of teammates by allowing me to punch him in the stomach to release stress. (He never laid a finger on me, even when my teenage angst destroyed our relationship.)

My mother also played a vital role in my early childhood. Despite being a workaholic pediatrician who probably had children for the wrong reasons, she fostered my intellectual curiosity and set my wandering mind aflame. She cultivated an early passion for reading and always answered questions I asked about subjects I was studying and made me proud to be a nerd.

But my parents had limitations that made them ill-equipped to cope with a sensitive, intense child that did not conform to societal norms or parental expectations. They never abused me, physically or emotionally. Many of the ways my parents have treated me over the years that I find objectionable are common for parents of their generation. But perhaps because of my eccentricities, their treatment of me made my life difficult at times and prevented me from growing up happy and secure.

My parents were both products of the Ozzie and Harriet 1950s and Nixon's Silent Majority and hated the counterculture they experienced during their college years. In my early years, my conservative father taught me important life lessons that many Americans have now forgotten, including that another person's malfeasance does not excuse your own (or as he said, "Two wrongs don't make a right"). I have taught my daughter many of the same lessons. But perhaps because he spent four years in the navy, he held fast to his ways of living and could never deviate from them, no matter how much my eccentricities caused him to lose any meaningful role in my life.

My mother's foibles would have harmed me even if I were not so different. To her credit, she was a tough, strong woman. She was among the first generation of women who fought their way into medical school and refused to listen when told she should be a nurse instead. But work always came first, then church second, and then only later came family. She was usually so exhausted by her other priorities that she had little patience for my sister and me. She expressed this impatience through tirades and needless attacks that were almost never followed by consolation or apologies, even when my sister and I were young.

After work, church also always came second for my mother, and it was not even religion, but singing in the church choir. She was a gifted alto who sang choral music while at college, and she prioritized her semi-professional singing career over family. The church also ruined many Christmases, as Christmases have been working holidays in my home devoid of significant family time since we moved to Florida, filled with rushed, brief, and unnecessarily formal Christmas Eve dinners, followed by hours at church on our own.

I would likely never have taken to religion. I never bought biblical stories and was always bored by sermons and the choral music my mother so adored. But my mother's obsession with her church choir (and the recent conversion of most churches to conservative political action committees) led me to detest all religion.

We were the stereotypical 1980s Reaganite family that was ridiculed by early 1990s alternative rock music. My mother had to have all the creature comforts that she thought made her happy. She could not have just a family, but also had to have a busy career, an exhausting pastime singing in the church choir, a boat, two kids, and a dog. She never understood that the more time you devote to one, the more the other is sacrificed, and kids are often sacrificed because they are harder than work or recreation.

My parents also never taught us how to have friends and, to my knowledge, never had their own friends. There were women we saw once a decade or so that we were supposed to call "Aunt," but my parents never spent time with neighbors or other people who lived in the places we lived. We also had little connection with other family members, even when we lived near them in Pennsylvania.

But that does not mean we were not made to pretend to be a happy family publicly. My mother hosted work parties, where my sister and I were forced to pretend to be happy, but as soon as the work associates left, the yelling resumed. I have bad memories of showing a fake face to the world and having the misery and fighting resume as soon as the cameras were off.

My real problems began when we moved to Florida the summer after I finished fifth grade. My parents didn't cause the problems I had during our first year in Florida. I now understand that I was just an overly sensitive kid as I am now an overly sensitive adult, and that nothing they might have done to ease my pain would have worked. But the move altered my life.

I might have managed the move better had we first landed where we settled one year later, in a suburb north of West Palm Beach. But we began our lives in Florida in a less civilized town, and it was a shithole. My sister and I still went to a private school, but it was nothing like the private school in Pennsylvania and was instead a snobby enclave for phony yuppies who didn't want their kids to mix with working class kids. The insular, *nouveau riche* kids that were there were hostile to outsiders, and I never made friends.

Baseball was worse. I was not prepared for how sports in Florida are not about fun but social Darwinism. In Florida, sports teach that it's a competitive world and losers need not apply. I had become depressed and overweight, so baseball, previously my greatest joy, became agonizing. I quit and did not play organized sports again until joining coed recreational softball and kickball leagues as an adult.

Life mercifully changed when my mother found a new job near West Palm Beach. Although I attended public school for the first time, I enjoyed it. Unlike the assholes in Prickville, most people near West Palm were northern transplants like us, and I was no longer the not-rich-enough new kid. I thrived in my classes and made friends. I also became happier after my parents enrolled me in the Boy Scouts. I enjoyed learning about knots, camping, hiking, and making fire. I also embraced my first experience in leadership, rising by my second year to Senior Patrol Leader after reaching the rank of Life Scout (the rank behind Eagle, which I never achieved). I loved nothing more than the merit badges, which were like mini college courses.

The Boy Scouts also introduced me to rock music. After my first meeting, another scout handed me three cassette tapes: *Dr. Feelgood* by Motley Crue, Skid Row's self-titled first album, and *Sgt. Pepper's* by the Beatles. They changed my life instantly. I immediately became obsessed with the Beatles, and I also loved hair metal, although that would not last. I enrolled in one of those 15-cassettes-for-$1 schemes and bought the crappiest late '80s hair metal: Poison, Nelson, Warrant—you name it. If an album had nine songs about getting wasted with strippers and a single power ballad for radio, I had it and perhaps liked it until 1991. To the extent new friends and Boy Scout merit badges did not ease the pain from my year in Assholetown, the Fuck You phony headbanging of men wearing pantyhose and mascara did the trick.

I also did my only backpacking until middle age as a Boy Scout. My first backpacking trip to the Appalachian Mountains of North Carolina was the best. My dad was there, and it's probably the last good memory we shared. Our troop spent the first week at the larger base camp earning merit badges, then spent a second week on the Llama Trek, where friendly llamas who didn't spit much carried our food and cooking gear while Boy Scouts and their adult leaders carried their tents and personal gear in backpacks. I suspect my dad knew it wasn't going to be easy. I was, after all, a fat kid who no longer played sports.

The first day was the worst. We ascended five miles, and I hated every second of it. It rained the entire day, I stopped every tenth mile, and my dad and I dragged behind the rest of the troop. By the time we reached the camp in a patch of trees atop a hill surrounded by a grassy field, the others had all pitched their tents and were relaxing. They took all the tent spots under the trees, and the only two unsheltered spaces left were in tall grass surrounded by low shrubs, one of which had a log of human shit right in the middle. We took the shit-free spot, and I continued to piss and moan about wanting to go home while my dad set up the tent and pretended to listen. I thought I'd never be dry again. But soon the clouds parted, the setting sun appeared, and my dad gave me a flannel shirt, and I became dry and better. Best of all, the next morning, my dad and I were the only ones that didn't have rain-soaked sleeping bags, as the grass lifted us from the streams of midnight rain that flooded the tents pitched under the trees.

I still hated the experience, even the day when one of the llamas got sick and a hippie we met on the trail cast some sort of hippie spell and the llama got up like he'd been touched by Jesus Christ himself (trippy). But one week after returning home, I wanted to do it all again.

Things got much worse shortly thereafter, and I have less sympathy for how my parents responded. My friends went to different high schools and depression returned, but this time my parents had had enough and were ready for me to grow up. Perhaps it was because I was less easy to live with. With rock music, puberty, and public school in Florida came rebellion and eventually those worst of sins, experimentation with cigarettes and sex. I had heated exchanges with my mother that were less weepy and more aggressive. But my parents did not help with their lack of empathy.

My parents were conservative, did not get out much, and hated people who did. It's not just that they never partied when they were young. They regarded with disdain people who do, the way country folk think city dwellers only destroy the world. They also grew up in a completely different time and place. Suburban South Florida in the early 1990s was not like the Ozzie and Harriet '50s. Kids smoked cigarettes outside my high school before class. Sex was not uncommon or frowned upon socially. Most kids did not care about church. My parents could not imagine such things. To them, only white trash was like that, and my parents have never understood or empathized with people who are not like themselves.

So when I began taking on the foreign characteristics of the vastly different world I occupied, my parents responded with intolerance and unfiltered castigation. My mother not only shat on every band I have ever liked and every sport I have ever watched on television, but even accused the women I dated of scandalously depraved behavior. I've always wondered if she thought I would be receptive to her attacks. I was not, and they exacerbated the divide between us.

My relationship with my dad also became unsustainable. He continued to serve as an adult leader in my Boy Scout troop, but it sucked being the only kid whose dad was watching everything I did and being the only one disciplined for trivialities. My dad's inflexible commitment to the dad playbook caused more angry fights, particularly on drives home from Boy Scout meetings, which never ended with resolution for either one of us.

It all came to a head after one of my last Boy Scout meetings. We had another big fight on the drive home, and he stopped the minivan about two miles from our house and told me to get out and walk home. Not wanting to put up with my mother when I got home, I remembered a flyer from school mentioning that children could flee unhealthy homes by going to their local fire station and asking to be taken to a "Safe Place." Instead of walking home, I walked to the fire station and was taken from my cozy suburb to a shelter in downtown West Palm Beach.

It was a shocking experience. The kids there had real problems. There were elementary school kids with bruises and junior high kids addicted to street drugs. There were emaciated teenage girls prostituting themselves to get by. About five minutes after I arrived there, I called my parents and asked for a ride home. I don't remember whether my parents were relieved or angry. I only remember that we entered "family therapy" shortly thereafter.

It has always fascinated me how I now have such a positive regard for psychotherapy despite how terrible my first experience was. The experience might have been better if I had gone to therapy alone, but all four of us went—me, my mother, my father, and even my poor sister. It quickly became apparent that the only purpose of therapy was to make me understand that I was the cause of all family problems. No one had any interest in hearing what I had to say, least of all the counselor. Therapy only made things worse, especially for my poor sister who was caught in the middle, like being strapped to a movie theater seat and forced to silently watch grizzly horror films once a week. I would not see another therapist until my junior year of college.

Despite my so-called rebellion, I never got into trouble, got decent grades, and found high school theater, where my knack for memorizing lines and coming up with characters made me stand out. I also attracted the attention of older drama women and had my first kiss, followed shortly thereafter by my first girlfriend. As would become the pattern in my life, I fell hard and fast and sought from her the love and acceptance that was not available at home. But she moved away at the end of the school year, and I thought I would never see her again.

The fall of my sophomore year was the first transformative period that made me who I am today. I joined the debate team and the staff of the school newspaper, thrived in both, and would lead them and the drama club in my junior and senior years. I bonded with the friend who also introduced me to cigarettes. Smoking was the final straw for my relationship with my parents, although one they were unwilling to do anything to punish or prevent.

The beginning of my sophomore year—the fall of 1991—was when I truly discovered music. I remember the first time I heard Nirvana's "Smells Like Teen Spirit" and Pearl Jam's "Alive." "Smells Like Teen Spirit" detonated like an atomic bomb that autumn and I loved almost every song on *Nevermind*. When I bought *Ten* shortly thereafter and realized that the video for "Alive" was recorded live at a show and sounded *better* than the recorded track, I was hooked for life.

It wasn't just that Nirvana's rage and Pearl Jam's despair so clearly sounded like how I felt most of my waking hours. Or that their music perfectly explained the disconnect between my parents' rigidity and my exhaustion from Reagan-era dismissal of nonconformity. Nothing I had ever heard sounded like "Teen Spirit" or "In Bloom" or "Territorial Pissings" or "Lounge Act," especially at maximum volume. Nothing I had ever been able to say or scream or break could so clearly express the emotions that I was feeling better than Dave Grohl's drums and Kurt Cobain's explosive guitar.

Sadly, Nirvana's music is still more important to me than my parents. I played "On a Plain" on my Walkman before theater performances. When I was hospitalized for suicidal depression several years later, I took home the January 27, 1994, *Rolling Stone* issue with Nirvana on the cover that I found during an art project. It remains framed on the wall of my man cave, above the guitar, amp, and distortion pedal I play at least once a week, usually daily. *In Utero* remains the most important album in my life, and I even signed my suicide note with lyrics from "Radio Friendly Unit Shifter."

As I approached high school graduation, my life at home deteriorated into an endless cycle of shouting matches. My mother constantly attacked my music, friends, life choices, and my failure to be more like her. My father remained the rigid disciplinarian who demanded that rules be followed without question and denied love when I refused. Nothing I did was ever good enough. When I pointed out that I was doing well in school and was a leader in multiple school organizations, he dismissed me by saying that every time I took a step forward, I always took three steps back.

My parents seemed to believe that my sister and I existed only to be clones of themselves—we had no independent identities worth recognizing. Had we grown up in their insular Ozzie and Harriet world, that might have been possible. But they moved us away from that world into one they had no interest in trying to understand. I was supposed to follow their demands blindly, but I'm just not programmed that way. I can't just agree with what I'm told, and I could never be a follower. Teachers or classmates never considered me to be a problem; I just question rules and resist the ones that don't make sense. As a result, I was blamed for every family problem, and my parents and I turned our house into a war zone.

By the time I left for the University of Florida in the fall of 1994, I was excited intellectually but knew I was unprepared socially. I was leaving trench warfare to live for the first time with a roommate. I had few friends other than a few scripts, Nirvana and Pearl Jam CDs, an acoustic guitar, and several hundred Camel Lights. The guy I usually smoked them with went to Florida State instead. I may have been scared, but I was glad to leave home and try to find a place where I belonged.

College was, with apologies to Dickens, the best of times and worst of times.

It began well, as I hit the jackpot with my freshman-year roommate. An award-winning body builder in high school, he looked like a baby-faced pre-*Conan* Arnold Schwarzenegger. He was also a genuinely nice guy, and we bonded from the get-go, going to rock concerts and even an improvised bus trip to Mardi Gras. We had lots in common, despite his outgoing personality. We enjoyed trying new things, we had poor residential hygiene, we loved to get fucked up, and we were nonconfrontational.

My roommate and I also shared stories about the fraternities we pledged. It still baffles me that I joined a frat, although the reason should be self-evident. With my introversion, I needed a ready-made social network at a school as big as UF. I also bought the bullshit about frats being helpful in getting jobs. Although I enjoyed it at first, the illusion wore off after I moved into the frat house during my sophomore year. All the guys I admired when pledging had graduated or quit after my freshman year, and most of the guys left were either wrestling-obsessed rednecks on the seven-year plan who wanted to cut all ties with sororities or political phonies. Worse yet, they drew battle lines in house politics and forced everyone to take sides, when all I wanted to do was make friends and meet girls who might sleep with an introvert.

Frat life was nevertheless the most important educational experience I had in college because of two key lessons I learned. The first was how terrible people can be to each other. People fucked each other's girlfriends and bragged about it at chapter meetings. One of my "brothers" tried to fuck my actual sister when she had too many beers while visiting from high school—I kicked down his door and dragged her out like a raving lunatic. I was also dragged into a political war between the rednecks and the politicos. Although I was stuck with the politicos, the rednecks had the numbers, the next year's incoming president, and the willingness to bully anyone who got in their way. Their opinion leader, a redneck with a barely understandable speech impediment, threatened to kick my ass several times. The politicos were weak and unprincipled, and when their leader defected to the rednecks to save his political future, I scheduled classes during dinners and chapter meetings. I had everything in my room packed in my car before my last final at the end of the spring semester.

I never stepped foot again in the frat house after moving out at the end of my sophomore year.

The other key lesson I learned at the frat was what squalor really looks like. The carpets were shampooed with beer and piss. By the end of the spring semester, people started pissing on the mystics in the chapter room to avoid walking the spongy floors to the bathroom. No one noticed. If I needed any motivation to study hard, that sewer pipe provided it.

On the bright side, I thrived academically and finally got straight A's the second semester of my freshman year after having a false alarm heart attack that I would lose my scholarship after getting less than a 3.2 GPA the first semester. (I was highly motivated when I realized I had one more semester to raise my GPA.) I had never earned more than three A's a semester in high school, but even as my depression worsened through college, I earned the best grades of my life.

I also found the greatest passion in my life besides angry rock music: Florida Gators football. My first game my freshman year blew me away. It was like a rock concert with rules—Yell like hell when we are on defense to disrupt the other team's snap count, but when our offense is on the field, shut the fuck up. It was also lucky to be at UF in the middle of the Steve Spurrier era. The Gators won three SEC Championships and one National Championship while I was at Florida, and the happiest day of my life before my daughter was born was my final home game my senior year when the Gators ruined Florida State's bid for a national championship, beating them by alternating quarterbacks on every offensive play. I have been to at least 130 Gator games in the years since and have had season tickets for 15 years.

Gainesville was such a different world than my parents' home. I went weeks without seeing anyone over the age of 30. The smartest girls I had ever met laid out by dorm-side pools six months a year in bikinis and didn't seem to mind when I sat nearby pretending to read. I could play guitar and see bands in three different cities less than two-hours' drive away. I loved my classes and double-minored in art history and business.

But ultimately, I was alone. I never found a girlfriend in my first three years at Gainesville, and I had no friends in my major of public relations, which catered more to the *Ally McBeal* crowd and dismissed me as a misfit nerd. I started seeing a campus psychologist, but nothing changed.

Things finally started to improve my senior year. I reconnected with my roommate in the shithole frat house (he had also cut ties) and tagged along with his social circle, and those five guys became my best friends. He and I moved into an apartment my senior year with another guy with a bigger circle of friends, one of whom had a pre-game party pad near Ben Hill Griffin Stadium. It was with those friends that I shared that 1997 FSU game, the last game I remember that we all attended together.

I also connected for the first time with my sister. She was two years behind me, and we hadn't attended the same school together since that private school in Pennsylvania. She hated me while we lived together (for good reason), but when I started bringing bottles of Jack Daniels home from college and venting about our parents, we began bonding.

She arrived at UF my junior year and hung out with me and my friends, eventually marrying one of them. We even took a class together. I had never imagined before that we would even talk; now she had become one of the most important people in my life.

And I finally found a girlfriend, a familiar one. Almost by accident, I ran into my girlfriend from my freshman year of high school, and we began dating shortly thereafter. Like all the women I've dated, she was a wonderful person. By then, I also decided to attend law school. I was still not yet ready to grow up, and three years more seemed like enough time. My grades got me into three top 25 law schools but notably not UF. I didn't mind, as I wanted to try a smaller school further north anyway. I fell in love with a law school in Virginia, and when I left Gainesville to go there, I expected to marry my girlfriend, who still had one more year left at UF before she also planned to go to law school.

Life was also the best and worst of times at that law school in Virginia, but with more life-shattering consequences. I did not stay for three years.

I arrived at that law school with confidence and quickly made a new circle of friends, and they were not only nice, but brilliant—all smarter than me, which was fine, I loved the stimulation. They also loved to drink beer, and some even played guitar. I performed with them in front of an audience for the first time at a class talent show at a local coffee shop.

What shaped the course of events there was romance. Shortly after arriving, I was smitten by another beautiful, brilliant girl. Although I thought I loved my girlfriend in Gainesville, I could not resist pursuing the new girl and sheepishly broke up with my girlfriend in Gainesville and immediately began dating the girl at the new law school. I still deeply regret the pain I caused my girlfriend in Gainesville, and not only because she handled the situation with class and dignity.

The relationship with the new girlfriend followed the same pattern as my other romantic relationships. I was moody and depressed, projected personality traits that were not hers, berated her when she failed to conform to them, and never got to know the real person she was. I also had a paralyzing fear of ending my time at that law school without meeting the woman I would marry, which further strained our relationship. She dated me for the rest of the school year, then politely but wisely ended the relationship before the summer following our first year.

I was devastated. I had fallen harder this time than ever before, and I panicked that I may not find anyone else to date again. I became hopelessly depressed and even strangely dissatisfied with my new friends. It didn't help that I had earned mediocre grades that landed me at the bottom half of my class. I would torture my sister by calling her late at night in depressed agony, then never call her later to let her know that I was okay. The ex-girlfriend showed great sympathy and kindness through the summer and early fall of our second year. But by then I was spending hours on overpass bridges at night, hoping to raise the courage to jump in front of a

Osceola National Forest, April 9, 2024.

moving car, and walking the gun racks at the local Walmart in the middle of sleepless nights.

Everything came to a climax in the middle of a September night during the beginning of my second year when a friend awoke to find me playing with a knife and bleeding superficially from my wrists. The friend knew I was depressed, and I was taken immediately to the school infirmary. Within 24 hours, my parents had arrived to drive me home and directly to an inpatient mental health treatment center. Whether I knew it or not at the time, my time at the law school in Virginia was over.

My first experience with inpatient psychiatry was frightening, as I knew nothing about it other than that civil commitment was historically permanent and hard to undo once initiated. Although I was told I could leave whenever I wanted, I became skeptical when the doors locked behind me, and I did everything I could to convince staff to let me leave immediately. After all, I wanted to die to get away from unrelenting hopelessness and pain, not continue to suffer indefinitely in isolation. I lied to the staff and told them I had never been suicidal, and I did everything I could to convincingly act the part. I was released the third day after arriving.

Predictably, things did not get better. I still had severe depression that had not yet been fully diagnosed or treated. Sleeping had always been difficult, but by that summer, I had started using melatonin every night, at first two pills at a time. I was eventually taking handfuls at a time. I also had to go back to living with my parents. I would not have improved anyway, but their initial sympathy turned to impatience about my lack of direction and guaranteed that things would only get worse.

Five weeks after returning home, my mother found an eight-page suicide note on the printer in my room, ending with those lines from "Radio Friendly Unit Shifter":

> *Hate your enemies*
> *Save your friends*
> *Find your place*
> *Speak the truth*
> *What is wrong with me?*

The rest was a diatribe about all the things my mother had done to cause my suicide. When my parents found the letter, I was immediately rushed back to the inpatient facility. I knew this time that I would not be out in three days. But I no longer cared what happened. As far as I was concerned, my life was over, and they could do whatever they wanted with me. I spent three weeks there this time, and they saved my life.

Indeed, I was *reborn* during those three weeks. I was once again initially frightened. The facility was a crisis center for the entire spectrum of mental illness. There were bipolar drug addicts fresh from detox working out their meds before returning to battles with addiction. There was the young mother with postpartum depression who could not bear to be around her newborn baby and had to be watched like a hawk around male patients to protect her from the irresistible impulse to have sex. There was the giant paranoid schizophrenic who had a hallucination that caused him to drive away from his home at over 100 miles an hour, striking and killing a family. He had a huge scar on his forehead that made him look like Frankenstein, but he was one of the nicest people I met there, and like the rest of us, his problems were far beyond his control.

Once I got past my initial fear, I understood how special that place was. Beyond receiving therapy from physicians and during group sessions and creative projects, I was also granted the freedom to smoke as much as I wanted to relieve anxiety. I was even allowed to have my acoustic guitar once the staff became convinced that I would not use the strings to harm myself.

I particularly loved the staff. Everyone there, from the orderlies to the nurses to the janitorial staff, were devoted to making you feel better and monitoring your mood. They got to know all of us, constantly checked to see how we were doing, and told us about the progress they were seeing. I had never remembered being around anyone who was so sensitive to my feelings, and now I was in a sanctuary surrounded by people who *all* cared about me—the *real* me, not just the me they wanted me to be.

The physicians who treated me during my three-week return to inpatient psychiatric care saved my life and taught me how to live. They recognized that although I had major problems with sleeping and was severely depressed, my larger problems were more basic. I had never developed self-esteem or learned how to have healthy relationships with other human beings, especially the women I dated. I searched for the love and acceptance I never felt at home exclusively from the women I dated, which is obviously a lot to lay on a girl on the first date. Having spent my life searching for an idealized image of the mother I never knew; I projected those qualities on the women I dated. This not only put unsustainable pressure on the relationships, but prevented me from getting to know who they really were. This also guaranteed that the relationships would suffocate under their own weight.

The first mission of my physicians was to sow seeds of self-esteem and teach me how to love myself. They introduced me to contentment, an emotion I had never experienced before, that comfortable feeling that has no thrill or excitement, but instead only safety and calm. I now seek contentment like a heroin addict searches for drug money under couch cushions. My physicians spent days trying to untangle everything fucked up in me since my childhood, including things I had fucked up in myself by filling in the blanks for how to live without knowing what belonged.

My physicians also understood that the only hope for me not relapsing was to stop the self-destructive pattern of relying so heavily on romantic relationships. They taught me that before I can date again, I must figure out who I am and become content with that person. I had to become complete and self-sustaining before I could share myself with someone else romantically, and I had to know that everything would be all right if the relationship ended.

I have not seen any of the heroes who treated me since shortly after I left inpatient treatment. I do know that the inpatient health facility shut down several years ago. But I am authoring this book today only because of the miracles that happened there and the skill of the people who treated me.

The one thing I don't recall having ever discussed during inpatient treatment was alcoholism. I certainly had used beer to help me sleep, numb pain, and build up the courage to harm myself. But that didn't happen every time I drank, and I have never suffered withdrawal when I stopped drinking or smoking. I had smoked marijuana in college somewhat regularly (never daily), but that ended when I left UF, and I had never tried any of the drugs known to be addictive like heroin, cocaine, or methamphetamine.

But that didn't matter to my mother. She needed something to blame for my mental health problems, and she chose alcohol. It fit perfectly with her puritanical judgment of the world. It also conveniently allowed her to paint me as the cause of my problems.

So at my mother's insistence, when I left the inpatient mental health treatment center after three weeks, I was sent directly to a rehab center. This foolish decision caused the most severe trauma I have ever experienced, and she is lucky I didn't kill myself there. I've tried over the years to find some way to sympathize with my mother's decision. I suppose she was just trying to do whatever it took to get me better. But the fact is that she was a physician, not just a parent, and she should have known better.

If you remember nothing else you read in this book, remember this: Never put someone who doesn't have a problem with addiction in a drug or alcohol rehabilitation center that is not "dual diagnosis" if that person is suicidal, especially if they've just left intensive medical care for their condition. Never.

Here is why:

The purpose and methods of addiction treatment centers, at least the ones that are not "dual diagnosis" facilities that treat both addiction and depression simultaneously, are diametrically opposed to those of facilities that treat suicidal depression. The purpose of inpatient treatment for suicidal depression is to nurture patients and take every action necessary to prevent them from giving up hope and killing themselves.

The purpose of an addiction treatment center is completely the opposite. Alcoholics refuse to admit that they have problems with addiction, so the main objective of addiction treatment centers is to get addicts to accept that they have a problem with addiction. This takes a lot of convincing, and many addiction treatment centers use brutal methods to accomplish this task. They force the other addicts into emotional gang rape group sessions where staff and other inmates humiliate each other by calling themselves out on all the lies they have told themselves over the years to convince themselves that they're not addicts.

The rehab where my parents sent me straight from inpatient psychiatric treatment used brutal methods that, although effective for people who are not suicidal and who actually are addicted to alcohol, were the worst thing to do to a suicidal person without an addiction to drugs or alcohol. Having just barely learned to cope with the pain I felt from breaking up with my girlfriend and leaving law school, I was repeatedly berated for hours in a dark room by a trained expert and untrained junkies who told me I was lying about my depression and had to be hiding some problem with addiction, otherwise I wouldn't be there in the first place. I immediately became suicidal and thought about nothing but ending my life while I was there.

Seven days into my stay, another patient took too many liberties tormenting me during a group session, and I tackled him and started punching him in the face. I found out later that he was ejected the next day for doing the same to another patient. I was transferred to a less fancy dual diagnosis center in an office building where the patients stayed at an apartment complex, shopped for their own groceries, and spent their evenings watching shows about addiction and fantasizing about scoring heroin. Several did and were ejected from the program. But I made it all 28 days without incident. I swore that I would never be forced against my will into addiction treatment again.

I also never trusted my parents again. My mother's reckless decision, in which she placed a flippant prejudice against people she hated over obtainable medical knowledge, caused me more pain than I've ever experienced since. It would also haunt me later in other ways that she can be forgiven for not having anticipated.

Despite all of that, I gradually improved. I easily refrained from drinking at my physician's recommendation.

I continued therapy and slowly learned how to deal with my mood swings. I began filling my days by voraciously reading the volumes of classic fiction on my parents' bookshelf and eventually began working at my mother's medical office. I even reunited with my friends from law school and joined them for spring break in Key West, after bleaching my hair and looking like Eminem's fat cousin—I still cringe when I see my sister's graduation pictures from that spring.

I also decided that I wanted to return to law school, but I knew returning to the law school in Virginia was a bad idea. I was inclined to return to Florida, and the only public law schools in Florida at the time were UF and Florida State. Normally a person in my predicament would transfer, but my grades were too low to transfer as a second-year law student to FSU, and I did not want to transfer to a lower ranked private school where I'd rack up oodles of student loan debt.

So I applied to Florida State's law school as an incoming student. I had never heard of anyone attempting this before, but with my unique circumstances, I figured it was worth a shot. I disclosed those circumstances in my application and explained my mental health problems. I reasoned that Florida State wouldn't mind accepting three years of tuition rather than two, and that they'd view me as a good risk because of my LSAT score and high grades at UF. It worked, and I started there the following fall.

My first year at Florida State was a resounding success in all ways but popularity. Because I was no longer drinking, I studied and outlined cases while others socialized. I had also gained weight recovering from depression, so I did not have to worry about dating my first year—the only girl I asked out politely declined. I had few friends, but I didn't mind. I was not at FSU to party, but to salvage my pursuit of a career in law. All that mattered to me was to have a decent job waiting for me when I graduated, and I had overcome too much to care about what people thought of me. I also put the nail in the coffin for any hope of popularity at FSU by being invited onto the *Law Review*.

The nice thing about being on the *Law Review* is that people recognize your name when they inherit the outlines they use to study for finals. A pretty student from the class behind mine used an outline of mine to study for a first semester final and was not put off by my looks when she recognized me studying in the library the following January. I asked her out in the most pathetically junior-high-way possible—through a hand-written note that I handed her between classes before sheepishly running away. She checked yes, and thus began the most important relationship of my life. We have now been married more than 18 years.

For once, I did not sabotage a relationship before it even began. Don't get me wrong, I was extremely attracted to her, but this time I took it slowly. I spared her for the first year or two from too many details about my history, except to vaguely refer to the fact that I was not drinking only because I had unspecified issues with depression. But I also told her that she would not hear the words "I love you" from me for a long time—not necessarily because I didn't feel that way, but because I'd ruined prior relationships by taking things too intensely too fast and I didn't want to do the same with her. She got it and didn't mind.

In other words, I applied the lessons my physicians taught me. They worked. She was the only girl I ever dated longer than one year, and we were engaged by the end of the summer after she graduated. I even convinced her to follow me to Orlando when I knew she wanted to return instead to where she grew up near St. Petersburg. Not only is she the kindest, most loving, most supportive person I've ever met, but also, she stuck with me after I told her the ugly details about my past and warned her that depression never goes away forever and will almost certainly return. I even made sure we were engaged for two years, to give her time to back out before the wedding if she saw the dark side and decided to spend her life with a safer option.

My wife also had a family I had never known, but always wanted. Her parents were interested in getting to know the real me, not just some preconceived notion of what they wanted for a son-in-law. Her brother was a cadet at the U.S. Military Academy who was Mr. Everything in high school— one of those born leaders that excel at everything they attempt and look like Adonis. Her older sister was as kind and smart as my wife and lived in a small town in Montana with a husband who was a family doctor who was just as kind and smart. Despite being good at almost everything they did, they were all the most humble, non-judgmental people I've ever met. I never showed them too much of myself or told them about my past—I didn't want to scare them off. But it was the first time I found a family that welcomed me for who I was. My wife and I wed three years after I graduated.

My career ambitions panned out. I managed to perform well enough at a summer internship between my second and third years of law school to earn an offer after graduation to join the commercial litigation department of one of Orlando's oldest law firms. But it was when beginning my career that my mother's ill-conceived decision to send me to rehab came back to haunt me.

When I began my career, the Florida Bar gave me the "choice" of either agreeing to a contract requiring me to comply with burdensome addiction-related terms during at least the first three years of my career or find a line of work other than practicing law. Even worse, virtually none of the onerous requirements had anything to do with treating mental health problems, but instead addressed perceived addiction problems. These included having to call a number every weekday to find out if I would be required to appear at a drug testing center during working hours to submit a urine sample; I would be notified of my need to appear five times a year on randomly selected dates. I didn't fear the testing, as I was still not drinking based on the advice of my therapists. But I laughed at the absurdity since the piss test could only detect alcohol consumed less than 36 hours before the urine sample was provided. This was the classic case of a punch-list bureaucracy finding a round hole for a square peg.

Most diabolical was the requirement that I see a therapist of their choosing at my own expense. That therapist reported directly to the Florida Bar, so I had no confidentiality. If I ever even hinted to this therapist that I was thinking about suicide, I would exponentially magnify my problems by jeopardizing my career, so that "therapist" was the last person I would have ever shared any thoughts of suicide.

I luckily never felt suicidal during that time, but the four years I spent complying with the Florida Bar contract amplified the already high amount of stress that law school graduates experience in their first jobs. The Florida Bar contract ruined what should have been an exciting time of my life, including my engagement and the first year of my marriage, and caused long-term damage to my mental health that I'm still coping with.

Otherwise, the beginning years of my career went well. I met a mentor who took special interest in me and chose me as his go-to associate. My wife and I began travelling to Europe the summer after I graduated and returned to Europe almost every summer thereafter until our daughter was born; we have also returned to Europe with her four times since. We also discovered the band that provided the soundtrack of my adult life—Incubus—and my wife and I have seen them in concert together more than ten times. I also finally bought an electric guitar and began playing ear-splitting grunge every Friday to get rid of residual stress from the work week.

My wife and I wed in St. Petersburg during my third-year practicing law. At the wedding, my mentor told me that he was leaving the firm to join a bigger national firm and asked if I wanted to follow him. I interviewed shortly before my honeymoon and began the new job in June 2006. The ten years I spent at this second firm made me the lawyer I am now. But they were not easy, and if there was ever a question whether my depression and anxiety would return, those years made it inevitable.

On the bright side, I finally made friends in Orlando. I played on the firm's softball team and began socializing with other associates outside of work, including female attorneys who I introduced to my wife and who often became closer to my wife than me. My wife and I also joined an adult kickball league and met a new bunch of great guys who also graduated from UF—engineers who enjoyed partying. Released from the Florida Bar contract, I was finally able to enjoy the occasional beer, and I started taking those annual trips to Las Vegas. Our team even won our league one season and earned an invitation to the national tournament in Vegas, and *that* was a shit show. We crapped out in the first round of the tournament, but we made the most of our time on the Strip and had a once-in-a-lifetime blast.

I also had professional success early at the new firm. I initially seemed to be regarded well by the partners, and I was eventually even asked to lead the summer associate program. It was implied that this would be a steppingstone for partnership. But the good times didn't last. Although most of the partners were friendly, some were more than just a little bit difficult to work with and seemed to hate me. The rosy treatment I received in the early years faded as I started approaching eligibility for partnership, perhaps because of pressure placed on the firm by the subprime mortgage crisis. My practice group also required its associates to take leadership roles in the local bar association and local charities, and even to attend expensive American Bar Association meetings for which I never received reimbursement. While we watched colleagues from other practice groups in our office focus only on work, the associates in my group were assailed for not spending enough non-billable time on community and bar activities.

In fairness, the requirement to participate in community organizations benefited me. That was how I joined Florida Citrus Sports and the local Gator Club, where I not only received awards for my leadership, but also made friends. Along with Gator football, my wife and daughter, and my guitar, these organizations allowed me to survive those years without feeling the need to return to therapy. But they all proved fruitless to professional success, as I was told when being instructed to not waste time applying for partnership that the hundreds of hours I spent on community and bar activities did not count because they weren't the right organizations.

To be clear, I don't think I was cheated out of partnership at that firm. I certainly cannot dispute that my peers who made partner were deserving. But I knew—as I suspect I realized long before I ever considered law school—that I had no hope of making partner at a big, political firm like that for the same reason that I was hated by popular kids all my life. Because of my eccentricities, I just wasn't the guy that was picked for those kinds of things. After ten years at that firm, I left for a smaller firm.

I thrived at the new smaller firm. I finally felt appreciated and didn't have to worry about making the right people happy. I was also finally relieved of any obligation to spend hundreds of hours doing non-billable work, although I still stayed involved with Florida Citrus Sports and the Gator Club. And despite working less than I did at the big firm, I was now exceeding expectations. In March of 2023, almost 20 years into practicing law, the firm made me a partner. I had now finally achieved everything I wanted from my legal career.

I still had some major ups and downs in my personal relationships. My relationship with my parents continued to deteriorate. It also suffered indirectly when my sister and I had an explosive fight while we were both visiting my parents during the Christmas of 2015—for once, my mother was a victim of collateral damage rather than the cause. My relationship with my sister had been deteriorating for years after she moved away from Florida, and the fight was so bad that I avoided contact with her for almost eight years.

But my marriage was fine, and being my daughter's father has always brought me more joy than I could have dreamed. My wife and I reveled as we watched her thrive first in dance, then in school and sports. Other than being massively overweight (I ballooned up to 285 pounds by the spring of 2023), my life finally seemed to turn out well. I had been out of therapy and off meds for more than two decades, and I had the career, family, and personal life I always wanted. Although I was prepared for the eventuality that depression might one day return, I now finally had a life less likely to induce it.

The author after weight loss, Withlacoochee Forest, Croom Tract, February 29, 2024.

The author before weight loss, circa 2022.

CHAPTER THREE

The Backpacking Fantasy is Born

T hen I lost more than 100 pounds and had to find a way to keep it off.

Actually, I had not yet lost *100 pounds* when I got the idea in December 2023 to try sleeping in a tent again for the first time in almost 35 years—at the time, it was only about 80 pounds. I wasn't sure how much longer I could keep walking five miles four times a week without getting bored. Besides, I wanted to play with the new toy I was now walking around in. After all, what's the point of losing that much weight if you don't have fun with it?

I had already begun sailing again, having spent summers and weekends in high school with my best friend sailing and flipping catamarans at a local resort while working for free for the small business that rented them. The sailing bug bit again when I started watching sailing videos on YouTube. After finding a sailing club that offered ASA 101 courses and the opportunity for memberships where 23-foot sailboats could be used by members who passed the course, I took the class in October and passed. This despite notably having a panic attack during my practical exam that should have gotten my attention but didn't. But I was not ready for membership and had to get more experience, and it was still football season anyway. I therefore needed to find another outdoor pastime. I began hiking regularly again, but it wasn't enough.

The dream struck like a lightning bolt during a trip in early December to Dick's Sporting Goods to buy a new bathing suit (it was nice to finally not have to buy them from big and tall websites). During a random stroll down the camping aisle, after seeing the big jumbo parking lot tents, I came across a single Eureka Solitaire AL in a box showing the tent *in situs* in the mountains. This wasn't like the parking lot tents. It was barely long enough for a single person to lay down in and had a rollback rain cover atop a curved canopy comprised almost entirely of transparent mosquito netting. Since my wife had put in our pool two years earlier, I had begun enjoying sunrises and sunsets. This seemed like the perfect way to enjoy them even more.

Of course, there were reasons to not waste the money. For one, I had never enjoyed camping as a Boy Scout because of Florida's mosquitoes and heat. I am genetically predisposed to sweating more than other humans. Family lore has it that my dad was once recruited off the street to play the sweaty guy in a Turtle Wax commercial but was replaced because he perspired too much. I was similarly famous for showering five times a day during those trips to Las Vegas. But the weight loss had reduced my sweating, and mosquitoes are rare in Florida during the winter—the only time when it's cool enough to camp anyway. The sleep apnea also abated significantly with the weight loss.

To be clear, I had not yet decided at that moment to try backpacking again. Even if I could sleep in the tiny tent, I did not think I was strong enough to carry more than 30 pounds of gear into the forest, then sleep in the tent after soaking myself with salt water into presumptive misery. Nevertheless, I saw a backpack with a well-padded hip belt just down the aisle from the tent, and perhaps I could build up to using it someday. I would never know unless I tried sleeping in the tent somewhere. Like many, I also enjoy an occasional impulse purchase. So I purchased the tent, the backpack, and a light, self-inflating air mattress as Christmas gifts and took them home and spent hours dreaming about the picture on the box. The fantasizing adolescent had a new dream.

I first had to see if I could sleep in the tent. I knew I had more problems than just heat, mosquitoes, and apnea to overcome.

Sleep has been a lifelong problem for me, regardless of my weight, age, or living situation. The bed has always been the least favorite piece of furniture anywhere I have lived. For my entire life, I've been unable to sleep anywhere without:

- A very cool environment (except in winter, when I strangely need a space heater to blast an absurd amount of heat instead),
- A ceiling fan or rotary fan to circulate the cool or superheated air over me constantly,
- A television with a sleep timer to distract the unquiet mind until it shuts up,

- Something else to create a buzzing sound over the TV if the fan is too quiet, and
- Sufficient thickness in blinds or curtains to block out all non-televised light.

All these sleep aids are even more critical when sleeping in hotels. After learning the hard way that too many European Vrbo's do not have fans or air conditioning, I now buy a cheap fan the day I arrive anywhere in Europe and strap it to the outside of my suitcase wherever I go. Even since my adventures in backpacking, I can almost never sleep at someone else's home, presumably because I'm afraid the occupants will find me ranting to myself in the middle of the night while walking around their kitchen.

This might not be too problematic, if I could just go without sleeping. Unfortunately, I cannot go without sleep, except on those rare occasions when pleasure drives me to enjoy as much time awake as possible (for example, in Las Vegas and on mornings arriving in Europe after sleepless transatlantic flights). Without sleep, I've never been able to take exams, argue effectively at hearings, or write motions or legal memoranda. The only thing I can effectively do without sleep is drive, but that's probably because I almost always have Nirvana or Incubus blasting at maximum volume. Not being able to get to sleep also drives me crazy and inflames my negativity and hopelessness. Which means if I can't get to sleep by three in the morning, I will remain awake for the rest of the morning no matter how tired I am *because* I haven't gotten to sleep yet. I start pacing the room and panicking about being unable to function the next day, even if I do somehow eke out two or three hours of sleep.

Losing weight had done nothing to change any of that, nor what I've now come to realize was a lifelong fear of the dark. So the last thing I was going to do was experiment with my new tent at a state park.

I therefore decided to try the tent in my backyard. Perhaps that's not unconventional. Kids have been sleeping in tents for years in their backyards. But I doubt too many neighbors see a grown parent of a pre-teen sleeping alone in his backyard in a tent the size of a coffin, especially in a yard as small as mine. I certainly worried about creeping out my neighbors, or at least getting "What the fuck are you doing?" looks. Weird as it may be, at least this way I could pull the rip cord and return to my bedroom if the ground was too hard or if sleep didn't find me by 2 a.m. I would also have a nice porcelain toilet with dry toilet paper walking distance away if dinner didn't agree with me.

After I confirmed there would be no rain and persuaded my wife and giggling daughter that I wasn't losing my mind, I set up the tent in my backyard on the Friday night after my purchase, with the door end facing the east to catch the rising sun, and I prepared for my first experiment sleeping on the ground since late puberty. I did not go unprepared. I had my iPhone and ear buds ready with Incubus and Nirvana on standby, as well as a flashlight and a book. I had a comfy travel pillow, an eye shade, and a pair of ear plugs from years of fruitless attempts to sleep on planes. I threw in an intoxicant or two to chill me out before I moved into the sleeping capsule. I even lucked out with unseasonably low temperatures in the high 40s to allow me to nestle deeply into my sleeping bag without too much risk of the sweat glands rebelling. Having become recently obsessed with *On Patrol Live*, I watched an entire three-hour episode to afford extra time to squeeze out the last drops from my bladder, before crawling backward on my knees into the tiny tent like an anal-retentive prisoner making a jailbreak through a sewer pipe.

When I finally settled into my sleeping bag and stopped squirming around, I found tranquility. The cushiony sleeping pad worked better than expected, especially on the thick grass in my backyard, so my back begrudgingly consented. To my surprise, the tight tent canopy did not feel claustrophobic, even though I had left the rain cover on and could not see through the netting. I had only inches between my sleeping bag and the walls of the tent, and it was certainly too confined to sit up or even bend much to loosen the zipper on my sleeping bag when it snagged my socks. But I was comfortable. It reminded me of how my parents explained that it was not cruel to put our dogs in steel cages at night because they felt safe inside the restricted space, as if in a den or cave. Without the space to rollover all night like a rock in a dryer, I felt more at ease.

After an hour or two, I fell asleep. Sure, I listened to an hour or two of ear-splitting grunge that probably kept the bunnies awake. But I eventually did fall asleep without air-conditioning, television, a ceiling fan, or blackout curtains. And it was heavenly.

The best part was that I woke up around 6 a.m., in time to see the sunrise—after attacking the tent zipper and pulling myself out of the tent like a newborn fetus on a tight schedule. Rather than go back into my house or even sit on patio furniture, I rolled back the rain cover, crawled back into the tent, and watched the sun break the horizon and crawl up the eastern side of our neighborhood while birds began chirping. I then texted my wife and asked for a cup of coffee.

I had passed the first test. Like all good scientists, I tried again the next weekend to confirm that the first run was not a lucky fluke, and the results were the same. I could actually sleep in a tent at age 47.

Now it was time to see if I could sleep in the *real* outdoors. There was only one place I considered for my first attempt.

For years, I had been hiking at two nearby state parks— Wekiwa Springs State Park and Lake Louisa State Park (*LL*). Lake Louisa had received most of my recent attention because of its closer proximity to my home. *LL* was also quickly becoming a sanctuary where I went to cope with inner demons, so I also had sentimental reasons for starting there. Perhaps most importantly, I knew it thoroughly. *LL* has more than 25 miles of trails through sandy pine and live oak forests and hills that are perfect for watching sunsets, and by the end of December 2023, I had been on almost every significant trail and could find my way around without looking at a map. *LL* is also more like a playground for outdoor enthusiasts than a nature preserve, as its trails cross paved roads frequented by cyclists. While much of *LL* feels nestled in nature, you never feel too far away from civilization, and I knew this would comfort me if a night alone in the dark spooked me.

There are also conveniences offered by state parks that are helpful for novice or born-again campers like me. Primitive campsites are often less than a mile from reserved parking spots that allow even parking lot campers to bulldoze in tons of supplies in wagons. Although I knew I was not going to do that, I did worry about the possibility that mosquitoes or sweat would drive me back to my car to sleep—I had spent many nights as a Boy Scout sleeping in my dad's minivan for similar reasons. So having the car less than one mile away on a trail I already knew reduced the risk that I'd get lost hiking back to my car in the middle of the night if the need arose. I also knew that a park ranger was a cell phone call away if I was harassed by raccoons or if I accidentally set something on fire other than firewood.

The only tricky part about camping at a state park in Florida in January is availability. Winter is the high season for camping in Florida, and campsite reservations during cold months at state parks near metropolitan areas in Florida can be hard to find. But demand is higher for RV and parking lot campsites than for primitive sites, which at $5.00 per night are also less expensive. The weekend I targeted was also the weekend after New Year's, which I correctly suspected would be less popular. It also helped that it rained several days that week. When one of *LL*'s two primitive campsites became available for the Saturday after New Year's, I immediately booked it.

At this point, the party planning committee took over. I decided immediately that I would not just camp, but instead do a decaffeinated version of backpacking with only about one mile in and out, but I did not want to risk being unable to carry backpacking weight even those short distances. Anticipating this, I had begun even before my sleeping-in-the-backyard experiments to increase my hikes at *LL* from 4 to 6 miles, and I started carrying the backpack with the tent, sleeping bag, and air mattress. I quickly realized that my legs had no problem carrying the added weight. After all, I had been walking around my neighborhood for months with far more than 40 pounds above my current weight; I was just carrying all of that added weight within my body rather than in a bag strapped to it.

As an attaboy for sleeping in the tent, I also rewarded myself with a small shopping spree at the local REI (Recreational Equipment, Inc.) store. I avoided for now the aisles with the freeze-dried dinners, as I was not yet ready to figure out how to safely use a backcountry stove. I instead focused on the basics: pocketknife, rope, bear bag, headlamp, Nalgene water bottles, insect repellant wipes, poncho, rainproof backpack cover, folding camp stool, and weatherproof bags for my food and clothes. Captain Boy Scout also threw in a small first aid kit. To keep weight down, I also bought a small titanium cooking pot and spork. I ignored the advice from the REI clerk to purchase a camp stove and instead decided to use the pot to heat canned chili over a campfire. And as always, I hit the book aisle and purchased two guidebooks on places to backpack in Central Florida, just in case I passed the first test at *LL*.

I also purchased what is now my backpacking instruction manual, Diana Helmuth's *How to Suffer Outside: A Beginner's Guide to Hiking and Backpacking*,[3] and I completed it before that first night at *LL*. (I highly recommend this book, as it is not just a great nuts-to-bolts how-to guide for novice backpackers organized by topic. It's also brilliantly witty and full of amusing anecdotes and important advice. It is therefore worth a read even if you have no interest in the outdoors. She is not paying me to say this [yet; cross fingers].)

On my way home from REI, I stopped at the grocery store to buy what I would eat and drink on my adventure. I had made up my mind that my first camp meal would be a Chunky can of chili, as a humorous tribute to the cold weather and the weight I'd lost. I also knew I needed coffee, and since I didn't want to waste time in the morning starting a fire when I'd rather be hiking at dawn, I went with a small can of high octane iced coffee. That also meant that I would settle for granola bars for breakfast. I also threw in a Gatorade for the hike in and a bag of M&Ms as a reward after dinner. None of this was recommended by Professor Helmuth, except maybe the M&Ms.

Over the Christmas holidays, I familiarized myself with the compartments of my backpack and decided what to pack and where to pack it. I also filled up my Nalgene bottles, picked and packed the clothes I would wear, and packed my bag so I could weigh it and see how close I came to keeping it under 20 percent of my body weight. This placed my limit just above 45 pounds. I came in right at the 45-pound weight limit for a single night in the woods, and I had not yet thought about the campfire. (For those not yet convinced that I had no idea what I was doing, the prosecution rests.) I also walked around my living room and back patio for half-hour stretches to get used to the weight and figure out the most comfortable alignment for the hip belt and shoulder straps. This built my confidence in being able to make it to the campsite and back fully loaded. It also allowed the neighbors to rest comfortably knowing that I had not yet regained my sanity after sleeping in my backyard.

I still wasn't ready to spend the night in the woods in sub-50-degree weather; we Floridians are a thin-blooded breed. I knew I needed to be able to start and maintain a campfire, and I had not done so in years. I was not willing to take lighter fluid, but I also wasn't ready to begin prepping for a *Naked and Afraid* audition by learning how to rub sticks together or cut sparks off a fire-starter with my pocketknife.

Here, my wife came in with a good idea for our patio. She had talked for some time about adding a fireplace to our pool deck. Although I hated the idea of a tacky propane contraption spraying tiny Silent Night flames around children's marbles, my wife sold me on acquiring a Solo Stove. As most Americans know by now, a Solo Stove is a take-anywhere fire pit that works safely on stone pavers, wood decks, or even short grass. It is so well-designed that even desk jockeys like me with comatose outdoor IQs can start and maintain fires within them and keep them lit.

I had a neighbor from Colorado who liked to host Halloween parties using a conventional firepit in his driveway, and he enjoyed playing with his axe. I invited him over the weekend before New Year's and had him host Man Class to re-teach me fire. I wish I had taken him with me to buy firewood, as I might have bought logs small enough to fit into the Solo Stove. I really wish I had consulted him before attempting to split one of those logs wedge-method by using a hammer and flathead screwdriver since I did not have a hatchet or saw. It did not work, and my wrists were sore for the rest of the week, especially after the screwdriver became stuck and I slammed the log on my patio for 15 minutes, childishly cursing like Ralphie in *The Christmas Story* while beating up the neighborhood bully.

The highlight of Man Class, especially for my daughter, was the neighbor's tutorial on axe usage after we both had more than one beer. While he pounded a full-sized axe like Thor inches from his thumb while squeezing the oversized logs between two feet clad only in flipflops, I squealed in terror each time I lightly tapped the single log I had practiced on for the 10 minutes it took me to finally split my twig. I let him keep his axe, and I now buy only smaller logs. A hatchet is wasted weight in a backpack anyway.

I passed Man Class and refreshed my memory on how to light and maintain a fire and move burning logs with a stick. Even better, I became familiar with the benefits of fire-starting briquettes and kiln-dried logs and kindling. I remembered how many times my troop of pyromaniac Boy Scouts struggled in Florida's humidity to light branches and pine needles found near campsites, and I realized that if I was really going to rely on a campfire to eat unfrozen chili, I should probably carry some of my Solo Stove fuel on the trail with me. It would take several trips to realize just how little I needed, and the amount I took on my first trip added more than 15 pounds to the outside of my backpack. (Amateur.)

Once I started planning my itinerary, I devised a way to avoid the added weight on the hike in. *LL* is a great place to watch sunsets from west-facing hilltops. Although the campsite

I booked was not close to any of those hilltops, a parking lot servicing the other primitive campsite was in between. After confirming with the park that I could leave my car for the night at the other spot, I decided to backpack in all my supplies other than my firewood and leave the firewood in the car. Then I would set up camp and leave everything in my tent other than a bottle of water, the headlamp, and the camp stool, and hike back to my car with those items in my backpack shortly before dusk. I would then pack the firewood in the empty backpack and leave it in the car while I hiked to a hill to watch the sunset with only the headlamp, water, and stool. I could then stop by the car on the way back to pick up the wood-packed backpack before returning to camp for a starlit dinner. I just had to not get lost in the dark.

I passed the test.

Everything on that first trip went better than planned, and I now recall almost every moment like a wonderful dream. The Pine Point campsite where I stayed that first time sits beside the trail and a quiet stream crossed by a small bridge, set among pine trees and blanketed with pine needles, with a big live oak spanning above the picnic table near the fire ring. It was easy to hang my backup flashlight like a chandelier over my outdoor dining room table. There was also a perfect spot for my tent far back from the trail in a clearing between the pines where I could roll back the rain cover and watch the stars if I could not sleep.

Campsite from first test at Lake Louisa State Park (Pine Point campsite), January 6, 2024.

Sunset from first test at Lake Louisa State Park, January 6, 2024.

The hike in was easier than expected, even though I was lugging 45 pounds and still getting used to my backpack. Setting up the tent and its contents took no time, and to avoid fumbling in the dark, I set up the chandelier, the bear bag, and a flat spot in the fire ring for the fire I'd start later. I even had around 30 minutes to rest with my spongy, sweat-soaked T-shirt hanging from the end of the picnic table. I shot back to my car early to drop off the backpack to have extra time to scout out the best hill to watch the sunset.

Beginning the adventure by watching the sunset was a good decision. For months, I had been disappointed by having to rush out of *LL* shortly before dusk to avoid being locked inside the gate (the rangers also drop by stragglers to provide polite warnings about park rules). I hoped for a pretty cloud-lit night, and my only disappointment was my inability to adequately capture the beauty I was seeing on the camera of my first-generation iPhone. I was completely alone on a small piece of paradise surrounded by brush and scrubby pine, looking over low hills and Lake Louisa in the distance, but I could not take my eyes off the sky. It was painted in slowly darkening shades of blue, orange, and white, and as I munched on granola while turning my camp stool every ten minutes or so to catch a different view, I hardly noticed when the horizon became so dark that it was time to strap on my headlamp.

The short hike back to the car for my firewood was even better. The trails are so wide and well-defined at *LL* that you rarely need to worry about losing your way. I therefore switched the headlamp to red light and focused on the emerging stars. I was so immersed in my stargazing that I hardly noticed the first rustling of bushes around me. Startled, I stood completely still and passed gas silently. Then once I got my wits about me, I began slowly scanning the red light strapped to my forehead like Rudolph's nose to the left, toward the rattling brush to see what was aflutter.

I had never remembered seeing many deer before at *LL*, perhaps because I had seen so many on morning hikes at Wekiwa Springs. I learned during my night hike back to my car that deer definitely live at *LL*, and not just a few. As I slowly scanned the red light strapped to my forehead 90 degrees to the left, I saw a pair of red eyes staring back at me less than 15 feet away. Then a second pair of eyes with the shadow of two backlit ears popped up nearby, like a target from an early generation Nintendo game. Several moments later, the first pair of eyes let out a big snort.

At that moment, the bushes and the trail in front of me erupted in clatter and movement. I never noticed the trampled bushes descending to a pond on the right side of this stretch of the trail when I had hiked there before. I now realized that this was a popular place where deer came to drink, and I had walked into a herd of them getting a drink. (By that, I mean if deer travel in herds. I am obviously not a biologist.)

Yes, I was initially scared, and I am sure I let out a few notes of profanity along with the air pollution. But as soon as I realized that I had now seen more deer at closer range in a split second than I'd ever seen before during an entire hike, I was awestruck at my good fortune. Story one for the wife had now been written. Minus the part about the farts and fear.

I tried my best to not walk too fast in my excitement back to my car and then to camp after picking up the firewood. When I got to camp and began preparing to cook my dinner, my excitement changed to intoxicating serenity, and I realized just how much I wanted to return to the trail to do real backpacking.

Primitive campsites in state parks are rarely far from other places where glampers and RV campers stay, but even though I was only a few miles from those campers, I felt like I was the last person left on earth. It was the most profound quiet I had ever experienced, and for the first time in my life, I felt truly alone. Between the spires of pine and through the boughs of the live oak, the stars shone down so brightly that the pines cast tall shadows over the contours of my camp. As much as I wanted to make dinner, I could not help but spend several minutes beside my tent staring at the night sky.

The fire and dinner preparation were easy. I had brought so much wood that I had no problem filling a square of kiln-dried logs with far too many broken pieces of kiln-dried kindling, and they ignited like the storm sewer in *Christmas Vacation* after I lit the fire-starter briquette with my Bic lighter. I avoided slicing my finger with the pop top lid on the Chunky can of chili (this was a pleasant surprise), and its contents heated to just the right temperature in no time in the titanium pot on the grill of the fire pit. I pulled the camp stool up to the picnic table and lapped up the chili mac and finished the last of my Gatorade before snarfing down the bag of M&Ms like Cookie Monster.

Then the real fun began. I had lots of firewood—way too much—and I saw no point in carrying any of it out or leaving any for the next campers. The fire thus lasted for hours. Having checked the anticipated wind direction and using the compass on my phone when picking my tent spot like the nerd that I am, I even managed to have a stream of smoke from my campfire pass directly over the front entrance of my tent. I presumed this would deter mosquitoes, but they were hibernating anyway.

Getting clean was particularly fun. As I mentioned before, I don't sleep well when sweaty or dirty, so I had purchased yuppies-only portable shower camp wipes from REI. The clerks must snicker at the dorks like me who purchase them. My tent is too small for changing or bathing, but I was alone in the middle of the forest. So after Hour 2 of my fire, I stripped down to my camp shoes and started wiping myself beside the campfire with the yuppie wipes, completely in *le buff*. I assumed a nice smoking would also cover any residual body odor, so I danced around the fire like an offensive Native American caricature as the deodorizing ointment dried. I liked it so much that I saw no need to put on clothes when the ointment dried. I therefore just stayed naked for an hour, hoping mosquitoes wouldn't be attracted to my nether regions or my Grand Canyon. There is nothing as liberating as prancing around a primitive campsite in the buff when mosquitoes are not biting. Let the raccoons think what they will.

I finally got tired sometime between midnight and 1 a.m., right around the time that the last kiln-dried logs had faded to embers. I wrapped up my boots in the tarp that had previously held the kiln-dried logs, placed the cover on my backpack to protect it from morning dew, and stacked them on the picnic table. I also placed my trash, remaining food, and other smellables in the bear bag. After covering the last orange embers with sand and hawking a few loogies on the remaining pile (again, not recommended by Professor Helmuth), I crawled into my tent and began the 20-minute wrestling match to find the perfect sleeping position.

Sleep came late, but not because of discomfort or the need to pee. It was because I could not take my eyes off the stars. They were so much brighter and more plentiful than in the backyard. Any fears of sweating in the sleeping bag also froze as the temperature dropped, and I pulled the drawstring of my sleeping bag snuggly so that only my face and ears stuck out. I also listened to the hoot of owls, which became more frequent and closer as the night wore on. When they sounded just a bit too close for comfort, I put in the earplugs, pulled my winter hat below my eyes, tucked my head inside the top of my sleeping bag, pulled the draw string, and fell asleep in a fetal position sucking my thumb.

More than an hour before dawn, I awoke with the predictable excruciating need to pee, and I crawled out of the tent into the chilly night and watered a pine tree, then jumped back into my tent in record time. Initial thoughts about going back to sleep faded as I listened to the owls (they were really at it now), and eventually I saw the first rays of sun fighting their way through the pines. This was no time to rest. I had seen my sunset. Now it was time to find my sunrise.

I got out of the tent, took down the bear bag, and took far too long to prepare the nearly empty backpack for my hike to the east-facing spot about two miles down the trail where I planned to eat breakfast while watching the sunrise. The delay proved fortuitous, as I started feeling sprinkles just as I started down the trail. I quickly rushed back to my tent and pulled down the rain cover. I then trod quietly down the trail through barely emerging light, hoping to not spook any more deer, but I did not see any.

I was particularly familiar with this stretch of trail. I had used it for weeks as part of a six-mile loop that circled two small lakes and passed beside the Pine Point campsite. The sprinkles stopped about 10 minutes before I reached the low hilltop where I planned to have breakfast. When I got there, I took out my poncho and spread it on the ground like a picnic blanket. I then took the coffee and granola bars out of the backpack, then leaned the backpack against my camp stool at the edge of my makeshift picnic blanket. I had what had to be the best table at *Chez LL* for watching the rising sun, and it even had a recliner to boot. I spent more than an hour lounging there alone. It was a fine way to begin the day.

I was in no rush to get back to camp since I had until noon to vacate the campsite, so I celebrated by taking the long way back by completing the six-mile loop. It was the most fun I had ever had hiking at *LL*, and I gleamed from ear-to-ear, greeting the hikers I saw on the trail like Howdy frickin' Doody. I discovered my first camping failure when I returned to camp and found the front of my tent soaked. I had forgotten to fold the tarp beneath the door of my tent to raise it above the ground and prevent draining rain from seeping in. But I still had plenty of time, so I hung the bear bag line between two trees and hung my sleeping bag, tarp, and tent to dry them out and hopefully avoid unnecessary water weight on the short hike out.

The first of many trail angels I would meet in the coming weeks greeted me as I finished packing. As I pulled the blue tarp off the line, I heard a soft voice asking for my attention. After initially ignoring it for reasons I cannot explain (Who else would they be talking to?), I raised my head and saw two horseback riders crossing the bridge beside my campsite, asking me if I could stop moving. I immediately realized that the tarp might spook the horses, and by inconsiderately ignoring their calls, I was risking having their horses buck them into the stream. To avoid distressing the horses anymore, I calmly but emphatically apologized and kept still as they passed. They were as nice as could be, asked me if my night camping had been pleasant, and thanked me for my tardy courtesy.

After carrying out my backpack, the still-soaked sleeping bag, and my trash wrapped in the mesh firewood bag hanging from the end of my firestick like Huck Finn's lunch, I threw the backpack in my car and drove to nearby Dixie Lake. I enjoyed my last swigs of water and bites of trail mix while sitting shirtless on the camp stool staring at the reflection of the sun off the water. I got in my car to return home and rolled down all the windows, and this time I turned off the earsplitting grunge and listened to the morning breeze.

I had passed my first backpacking test. Now it was time to start dreaming about what I would do next.

Florida National Scenic Trail at the Croom Tract of the Withlacoochee State Forest, February 29, 2024.

CHAPTER FOUR

Depression Returns and a Crisis Begins

B y the time I passed my first test at *LL*, my depression had already returned and was beginning to jeopardize my well-being and relationships with my closest friends. It would soon become even more severe and would impair my ability to work.

In retrospect, I should have seen it coming sooner. As I mentioned before, I began losing weight only after going two days without eating following a minor dispute with my wife, after the conflict appeared to have been resolved. For those two days, I was hopelessly negative, seething in anger more than depressed. I could barely get out of bed that first day despite not having a fever, and I could think of nothing but the earlier fight and could not get it out of my mind no matter how hard I tried. Most notable was the complete absence of an appetite, which does not happen very often for a 5'11" male weighing 285 pounds who watches six hours of television a night. Mental health physicians might characterize that two-day period as an episode of melancholic depression.[4]

Despite my weight loss in the following months and its gratifying impact on my mood, there were other signs that depression or something worse was returning. I had an explosive fight with a friend less than one month later and avoided talking to him for the rest of the summer. Because he was the only person that regularly went to Gator football games with me, I obsessed all summer about making alternative plans for each of the seven games I planned to attend, even though he presumably had no clue that I was still mad following our reconciliation the day after the fight.

I had a bizarre fight with my wife during a transatlantic flight to Amsterdam shortly thereafter, where I misconstrued a facial gesture that she made while we were attempting to communicate silently across the aisle of the plane. I exploded silently and communicated my rage through hand gestures, like a deaf psychopath signing threats to his worst enemy. I calmed down just enough before we landed to begin our vacation. I lost control of my temper again when we arrived at the central train station in Amsterdam and, hot and sleep-deprived, lost the train ticket needed to navigate through the station and its detours caused by construction. I became so impatient trying to get out of the poorly ventilated luggage locker room that I stomped ahead of my wife and daughter beyond their eyesight; I made a wrong turn and walked the wrong way out of the train station. I was then unable to get back in without my train ticket. My wife and daughter were left wandering outside the train station for an hour trying to find me while also sleep-deprived. We eventually reunited and made up and began one of our best vacations ever in the ensuing week without further incident.

There was also the two-week bout of downers in August that concluded with another two-day period of no energy or appetite. That was concluded by a disturbing encounter with a rude door-to-door solicitor who ignored our "No Solicitations" sign and almost tasted my fist. I left the next day for a trip to Salt Lake City for a Gator football game. When the flight landed an hour late and the car rental agency was closed, I was not polite to unhelpful staff at the car rental counter and barely held it together enough to find an alternative rental car. But at least I did not explode that time.

There was also the one weekend that my Gator football friend and I went to a game together—our annual weekend pilgrimage to Jacksonville for the Florida-Georgia game. For years, we had spent the weekend at a hotel on Jacksonville Beach and partied the night before at beach bars with alumni in tacky football shirts and drunk college kids in skimpy Halloween costumes. Having by then lost almost 70 pounds, I looked forward to this weekend all summer, despite the lingering issues with the friend. But we had several major conflicts, and although I did not become depressed, I left not caring if the friendship continued.

I also had conflicts at work which, although not unusual, now seem worse in retrospect. The practice of law and particularly litigation is not for the thin-skinned. Opposing attorneys can be vicious, and clients can be worse. The conflicts were bothering me more, and I was taking them far more personally—particularly attacks from clients who seemed to punch below the belt when disliking advice that they needed to hear. Even though I had the silent support of my firm, I was starting to feel unappreciated by my clients, and I believed civility was dying. At the time, I attributed it to the way our country has changed because of the deterioration of the political climate.

I should also have paid more attention to the music I heard in my head and how I was playing it on my guitar. As the soundtrack of my adult life, Incubus' albums have always been what I hear when enjoying the good things in life—trips to Europe, Florida Gator victories, sunrises, sunsets, winning hearings, or obtaining good results for clients—and Nirvana plays mainly during tough times. By August, Incubus had been relegated to the back burner, and I had begun playing Nirvana so often that I began instinctively avoiding all songs on *In Utero*, especially "Radio Friendly Unit Shifter." I had also rediscovered Our Lady Peace's *Clumsy*, an album full of sad and angry songs about depressed or mentally ill people who the world doesn't care about. What's more, I was playing "The Story of 100 Aisles" and "Big Dumb Rocket," the angriest songs on the album, with such ferocity that I was breaking guitar strings far more frequently than usual. It was all so cathartic that I thought this was keeping me healthy.

Aside from the broken guitar strings, none of this was particularly unusual, and none of it prevented me from functioning. I was still obtaining good results for my clients. I was still working the same number of hours, and exceeding work expectations enough to earn a substantial performance-based bonus as I had in prior years. I still fundamentally liked what I did for a living. My family life was great, and my wife and I had become closer than ever after resolving a conflict earlier that January with a heart-to-heart conversation about how to improve our relationship. That conversation and my resulting change in behavior led directly to a greater intimacy than we had felt in years, even though we'd never been very distant before anyway. I still loved playing guitar, watching Gator football, reading, and writing. Perhaps the joy I felt from the weight loss led me to accept these new problems as the price of mood changes caused by my changing body. At the time, I was willing to accept the bad with the life-altering good.

I had also endured one hell of a lot worse. These times were not as difficult as the ten years at the big national law firm, or the stress caused by the Florida Bar contract. They were a picnic compared to the issues I endured for decades with my parents. I had reduced my contact with my mother to several texts a year once Covid hit, only three months after an unprovoked attack in which my mother called me an asshole while somehow blaming me and all other men for a car accident that severely injured my brother-in-law hundreds of miles away. I had survived all of those without even considering returning to therapy, as I had been strengthened enough by my treatment at the inpatient mental health treatment center to survive everything life had thrown at me since 1999. If I could live 25 years after a suicide attempt without meaningful emotional support from my parents, I had no reason to believe that I couldn't make it the remainder of my life without more help. And now that I had lost weight, it seemed my life might continue happily a few decades longer than expected.

The problems finally began getting my attention in early December. I had made insulting, provocative comments on two separate occasions to two separate friends who had not provoked me first. Neither seemed particularly offended, but I was bothered by my behavior and could not figure out why I said what I said. The more recent comment was made moments before the friend's wife, one of my wife's closest friends, told us that she was pregnant.

The following day came the first of several events that unraveled me. Three of my four remaining best friends from UF had planned to get together at one of their homes during the week after Christmas, at the suggestion of the friend who now lived out of state but was visiting family nearby. That friend and I had gone together to the Gator game in Salt Lake City, and I had felt particularly close to him that weekend and shared with him that I had lost weight in part by virtually eliminating my beer consumption. The get-together the week after Christmas was to be a family affair, as my out-of-state friend would be bringing his wife and daughter, but my wife and daughter were scheduled to be out of town visiting her parents. I would therefore have to go alone.

My UF friends and I always enjoy beers when spending time together, and my wife would typically be the designated driver for such get-togethers. But without her to drive me home, I was hesitant to attend because I was unwilling to drink and drive. The host offered to let me stay at his house. But after initially welcoming the invitation, I began worrying about my ability to sleep there. I also knew that the host enjoys cooking. None of my friends hate broccoli, and I had a bad experience with one of the other friends from UF when I'd spent the night at his house after a similar get-together and he'd gotten a tray of the world's most foul-smelling broccoli, and I had to spend the entire evening alone on his patio.

(I hate broccoli—more than anything else in the world. More than boy bands, *Friends*, drivers who don't pass in the passing lane, people who tell you to not swear, or people who post videos on social media of themselves singing Disney songs while driving. My wife has agreed to never eat broccoli in my home if I will be there in the ensuing 36 hours. Even my wife's mother used to warn me before cooking broccoli in her own kitchen when we visit, to allow me to go for a walk and avoid explosions that she has never seen but has been warned about by my wife. She is a cool lady. But broccoli sucks.)

I texted the host to ask if broccoli would be served. I also hinted that I worried about the wives micromanaging my speech, as they are less tolerant of crude language than anyone else I spend time with outside of work. I suspect his response was not provocative. But I construed it negatively, perhaps unfairly. I will never know because I deleted the text messages.

The next day, I texted the friends to say that although I really wanted to come, in part because I was excited to tell them about my weight loss and my growing backpacking fantasy, I had to skip it because I was unwilling to drink and drive but could not safely count on being able to sleep away from home. The out-of-town friend asked why I had to drink. Or perhaps he suggested that none of us drink, or that he would not drink. I will never know because I deleted the texts shortly after receiving them.

I detonated. I construed his comment as a cheap shot about drinking, suggesting that I had a drinking problem. I took the comment personally because I thought he knew about the harm caused by my mother's decision to send me to rehab after I tried to kill myself. I also took the comment personally because of the special time I had with him several months earlier in Utah, and the fact that I thought he was above such cheap shots. He is also religious, and I assumed his inspiration for the perceived attack was evangelical Christianity, which I could not tolerate. I had always feared that his religious convictions and my aversion to all religion would drive a wedge between us. I decided at that moment that it finally had.

I did not tell him any of this at the time. I instead texted him and suggested only that there were more polite ways to tell me that he thought I had a drinking problem. And that I was therefore deleting his phone number. I did so immediately after sending the text and blocked his number. He sent an apologetic email later that day that I chose to not read for three months.

I also texted one of the other friends and asked him to find out why the out-of-state friend made the "cheap shot comment." When he responded by saying he was buried at work but also apologized for saying *he himself* was happy to not drink, I apologized for interrupting him at work and told him not to worry about it. He had been my friend long enough to know when I was irrationally and uncontrollably enraged, as I had been that way with him before.

I also deleted all text messages with all three friends and asked my wife later to text them separately to ask them to not include me in any future texts because I "was busy with work." I later deleted and blocked the phone number for one of the other two UF friends.

This all happened on the Tuesday before Christmas. I tried to distract myself with work, but I could not focus or think about anything other than the comment about drinking that I construed as the most offensive comment ever made to me by anyone other than my mother. Fortunately, work was slow that week, so my assistant had no concerns when I told her I was feeling sick and needed to take the rest of the day off. With Christmas right around the corner and most of my clients and opposing counsels out for the rest of the week and the following week for the Christmas holidays, I had no problem taking the rest of the week off, as my hours were high enough and I had never taken a Christmas vacation because I hate Christmas.

When my wife got home from work, she could tell that something was very wrong. I tried to explain, but I was ranting so incoherently that she could not follow what I was saying. I started weeping uncontrollably, as I had done during our heart-to-heart conversation about our marriage eleven months earlier, but I doubt any of it made sense. We went back and forth for hours, until she made the mistake of suggesting that I consider "seeing someone."

I was not ready to hear this, certainly not from her, and this was the only moment that day that my anger was deflected from my friend's comment and now aimed directly at her. I was attracted to my wife because she's never had any of the problems I have. She is positive, loving, optimistic, and well-grounded. She rarely loses control of her emotions, and on those rare occasions when she does, she is tearful but looks for resolution and does not get angry. Most importantly for this part of our conversation, she has not had much experience with psychotherapy. From my point of view at that time in my deranged state, she didn't know what the fuck she was talking about.

The bigger problem with her comment was that I construed it as her trying to pawn me off on someone else because she no longer wanted to help me. I impolitely suggested that she immediately "get the fuck out of my face," and when I calmed down enough a few minutes later to apologize and communicate more politely and with only a hint of greater clarity, I told her that you can't suggest to someone in such distress to go get psychiatric help. I was once again construing the comment as a below-the-belt cheap shot by one of the few people on earth who knew how much it would hurt my feelings. But at least this time, I understood shortly after erupting that my interpretation of her comment was misguided.

God love her, she calmed me down enough that we could now let the neighbors sleep (this all occurred on our back patio). I had a beer, finally got my pulse down, and became sleepy. After several hours watching the stars alone while ranting to myself as quietly as possible, I went to bed and slept a few hours.

The next morning, I woke up at 5:00 a.m. and could not get back to sleep. I would not sleep again past 5:00 a.m. until late March. And I was still seething, although fortunately capable of being civil to my wife. I also apologized to my daughter.

Work was out of the question, and I called my assistant again and told her I needed to take the day off because I was still sick. I hoped that I would lose my appetite and my energy, but the energy did not abate, even though the appetite disappeared. I had been hiking every weekend for more than a month at *LL* and had recently started adding significant weight to my six-mile hikes. This time I dropped the extra weight but knew I would be hiking more than six miles. I made a beeline to *LL* mid-morning after grabbing water and trail mix. I may have also grabbed lunch, but I doubt it.

I set off on the trail without having any idea where I would go. I found myself going to the deepest parts of the park that I had never visited before, to trails that had not been mowed for weeks. I found the tallest sand hills with the most porous sugar sand and ground up them without slowing down. Anytime I saw another hiker on the trail, I doubled my speed and passed without looking at them, not wanting them to see my tears. I ranted aloud to myself the entire way, trying as hard as I could to get out the rage and pain seething inside me. None of it worked.

Knowing already that I planned to camp at one of the park's two primitive campsites, I trekked to both and stayed just long enough to scout out potential tent sites. I then visited the primitive horse camp, then circled back the opposite direction and climbed several of the west-facing hills to scout

Florida National Scenic Trail at the Croom Tract of the Withlacoochee State Forest, February 29, 2024.

potential sunset viewing spots. But none of it made me feel better or exhausted my energy enough to go home. I finally began crashing at the top of the last hill and rested for some time, still unable to stop thinking about my friend's suggestion that I not drink. Self-harm never crossed my mind, it was only anger, rage, and pain. But I wanted to never talk to any of those friends again.

I don't know exactly how far I hiked that day, as I deliberately chose to not track my mileage. But when I got home and studied the map, I knew I had gone at least twelve miles and likely went as many as sixteen.

I was finally civil to my wife that night and apologized for my behavior the night before. She accepted the apology and did her best to help me. But I was still inconsolable. I again could not leave the patio for bed until 2 a.m.

I woke up again at 5:00 a.m. the next morning and was again unable to go back to sleep and instead watched TV until the sun rose. My legs and feet were sore, but I knew I did not want to brood at home in front of my daughter. I returned to *LL* again when the park opened and hiked another six miles. I was finally getting tired.

When I returned home and began fatiguing, the rage and racing thoughts subsided and were being replaced by deep despair, mourning the end of the relationships with three of my four best friends, who presumably knew nothing other than that I was irrationally angry. They had seen it before and presumably had no reason to believe this was any worse. I no longer cared to know anything more about their get-together, even though I could think about little else. But with despair came greater clarity and a better ability to communicate with my wife. We had a holiday trip to a hotel at St. Pete Beach scheduled for that weekend that I had been looking forward to for months, and I thought sunsets and afternoons relaxing on a quiet beach would help me get better.

I also agreed to return to therapy and to look for a counselor as soon as we returned from the Christmas holiday.

The weekend in St. Pete Beach did lift my spirits a bit, and we had good times. But it was tainted by misconstrued comments and hours of heated tearful and at times angry missives with my wife, where I could not be consoled or even figure out what I wanted from her. The worst was on Christmas Eve, where I went back and forth with her for hours on the balcony of our hotel suite. I eventually apologized, and we spent the rest of the night holding each other on the living room couch, while one or both of us whispered that things would get better. I'm not sure either one of us knew how soon that would be. I held it together long enough to salvage Christmas morning for my daughter. My wife cancelled her week with her mother and returned home with me and my daughter to care for me.

I resumed working from home, and the light week of work allowed me to pace myself. We found a therapist and scheduled an appointment for the week after my first test at *LL*. But my despair only slightly abated and was aggravated by a pending visit the weekend after Christmas by my parents that I had been dreading for months. Rather than cancel it altogether (it was my father's birthday), I prepared by hiking another six miles on the morning of my mother's arrival. I managed their visit well until I became visibly agitated by comments she made. My parents quickly suggested that they needed to get home and left before an explosion occurred. I mentioned nothing about my recent mental health issues, and this was the first time my parents had learned about my weight loss.

Work went reasonably well the week after the New Year's holiday and was a comforting distraction. The joy-filled trip to *LL* for my first backpacking test the following Saturday also deflected my despair, but only briefly. I met with my therapist and liked her immediately, and felt better after meeting her.

But I just could not stop thinking about the fight with my friends from UF. I had initially hoped that once the date of their get-together passed, I would stop being so upset and would finally become distracted with work or other family developments. But the day of the get-together came and passed, and still I continued to brood. My lurking anger and despair persisted, and now I knew I could not control it. I also still could not sleep past 5 a.m., no matter how late I went to bed.

Then problems at work took over.

One of my cases was becoming problematic because of an issue I did not cause. For reasons that I still cannot understand, a manager was angered by my advice, and after initially refusing to hear it at all, accused me without foundation of inappropriate conduct in an email copied to my boss that went *far* below the belt. Once again, I was deeply hurt. And enraged. I responded (only to my boss) with defensive emails supported by documentation that were far longer than necessary. None of it made me feel better. I again could not concentrate on anything but the incident that had upset me. I took the rest of the day off, then hammered out another five miles walking that evening in my neighborhood to relieve stress in my dorky Tevas with socks. None of it worked, and I felt worse when I returned than when I had started walking. Alas, I now finally had something to distract me from the anger at my college friends. I had another night of less than three hours' sleep.

When I woke up the next morning, I was still raging inconsolably about the client issue. I now felt nauseous and excruciating anxiety when I thought about *any* of my cases, and feared similar unfair criticisms in those as well. I felt mistreated and unappreciated and that no one cared. I lost faith in my purpose as an attorney or any hope that my clients would appreciate me and questioned how many ever had. I began thinking of all the times in the past six months when clients had responded unfairly to unwanted advice, and I replayed each word of each communication repeatedly in my mind while I rolled in bed before six in the morning.

I called in sick that morning (a Thursday), and I knew before I even went to bed that night that I would not be working the next day either. My assistants knew me well enough to see that this was not typical client-related frustration, and they were not surprised when I again called in sick on Friday morning, especially when I also told them I would not be able to check any emails until the following week. I also confirmed with my boss that I would reconnect with him that Monday.

By then, I had not slept more than four hours in a night for almost a month.

When I finished exchanging the text messages with my assistants that Friday morning, I hoped that a weekend away from work following two days "home sick" would clear my mind and allow me to resume working as normal; I think I told them that. I told myself that a regular weekend would allow me to have a good rant or cry and begin getting on with life. Worst case scenario, I could have a heart-to-heart with my boss about reasonable boundaries to set with my clients' case managers. But for the first time in my career, I began fantasizing about walking away from the practice of law and finding a new career where I could both enjoy my work *and* avoid people who made the work impossible to enjoy. I also hoped that I could finally stop thinking about the conflict with my college friends each moment I was not thinking about work travails.

I also had something coming up that I thought might just make me feel better.

Hike in during final exam at Lake Louisa State Park, January 19, 2024.

Campsite from final exam at Lake Louisa State Park (Wilderness Point),
January 19, 2024.

CHAPTER FIVE

Passing My Final Exam

$\mathcal{G}$ cannot remember whether I booked my second backpacking test trip before or after the crisis at work. I do recall that I found a lucky opening on a Friday at the other primitive campsite at *LL*, and I may have booked it before the unhinging client conflict, but it may have been the day after. I certainly committed to planning my final exam almost immediately after I passed the mid-term at *LL* on that first January weekend. I knew I needed to confirm I could hike with twenty percent of my weight longer distances on unfamiliar trails, so as early as the weekend before my crisis at work, I returned to *LL* and came up with a shorter version of my regular 6.5-mile loop, in order to have a more challenging 4-mile hike in with gear and a 2-mile hike out. I identified the ideal parking spot and confirmed with park rangers that I could use it.

What is certain is that two days after the panic attack that sent me home from work for the rest of the week in mid-January 2024, I returned to *LL* for a follow-up one-nighter that I now consider the last test for the solo backpacking trips that came shortly thereafter. The big work-related panic attack obviously put that trip in jeopardy. I was not going to risk ruining an adventure in the woods by being too emotional to focus or by risking my safety. My wife also needed to feel comfortable, and I suspect she may have worried about me deliberately harming myself while there. But I knew, perhaps intuitively, that returning to the forest was exactly what I needed. It had helped before when I had the crisis with my college friends.

I knew that getting into the woods, where I could pretend to be too far from cell phone reception, would allow me to feel at ease completely disconnected from the outside world. It also didn't hurt that I could now arrive at *LL* sooner to give me more time for the hike in and avoid rushing if the longer hike with gear was harder.

Even before the work crisis hit, I knew that this was intended to be a dress rehearsal for local backpacking trips. At that time, it was still less than halfway through Florida's winter backpacking season. I hoped I could find state parks less than two hours away with primitive campsites unreserved during at least one or two weekends before temperatures turned warmer in mid-March. Having purchased guidebooks from REI, I had several ideas for where I wanted to go next for weekend trips, even before the crisis at work hit. I therefore had plenty of ways to focus my thoughts on a more pleasant future. As it turned out, planning that second trip was the only way I could stop obsessing about work and my college friends.

I planned for the final backpacking test at *LL* in the same way I had planned the first trip. I still had all my supplies from the first trip except food and firewood, and I felt no need to replace any of what I had used the first time. I still put off learning a backcountry stove and opted again to cook Chunky soup over the campfire. I opted again for iced coffee and chose a more potent and nastier version that I presume is still awaiting FDA approval. I also grabbed more granola bars from my pantry for breakfast.

The big difference was that a cold front was moving through that Friday, so I had to prepare for temperatures in the low 40s. As I mentioned before, we Floridians cannot handle the cold, even northern transplants like me. My hands had been cold inside the sleeping bag during the first trip. So I took gloves and a neck gaiter with my winter hat and a winter jacket that I had not worn since exploring glaciers during a family vacation to Iceland.

This meant that I needed firewood again, and not just to cook—I would need it to stay warm before I became tired enough to sleep. I wrapped up the same 15 pounds worth of firewood that I had the first time. (Again, amateur.) My initial plan was to carry it with me on the four-mile hike in, and I took an old guitar strap and tied it to the bear bag line that I had wrapped around the tarp holding the firewood. But predictably, I could not find a comfortable way to carry this ridiculous contraption while also wearing my 40-pound backpack. So I had to make multiple trips once again. This time I chose to carry the wood in first, by stopping at the parking spot reserved for the campsite before my hike in. I then ferried the firewood in the half-mile distance from the parking spot, hiked back out to my car, and drove to the other spot to begin my four-mile hike in about three hours before sunset.

The hike in was the first time I started feeling like a backpacker, perhaps because I had not looked very closely at the weather before leaving. I had known that a cold front would move in that night. That was part of the attraction because I thought I would sleep better in colder weather. But despite having earned the weather merit badge back when I was a Boy Scout, I forgot that cold fronts often come with rain. Although my hike in started out sunny and hot, the sky turned dark right after I had completed the first mile, and it started to rain. And it did not let up until I was less than half a mile from camp.

It did not matter. As soon as I felt the first sprinkles, I pulled my back cover and poncho out of my backpack and put the back cover on my heavy luggage. But I was sweating profusely, so I paused on the poncho and instead clipped it to the outside of my backpack. The low rain clouds brought much needed shade, and the cool winter rain provided air-conditioning that would have been negated by the poncho, so I left it off. Alas, I was now comfortable despite carrying 40 pounds. I also had done a decent job planning a route without sugar sand, so I had a comfortable, solid trail under my feet the whole way. I did not just survive the experimental hike in. Even though I hiked twice as far with twice as much weight as I ever had before, I savored every minute of it.

I also moved quicker than expected and completed the four miles in less than an hour and a half, not much longer than it would have taken me without gear. This also afforded me the luxury of time to let my campsite dry a bit before setting up my tent. When I got to camp, I took off my backpack and set it on the bench of the picnic table, hung my wet T-shirt from a nearby tree to dry, had a nice satisfying whizz, set my camp stool atop the picnic table, and surveyed the nearby terrain for almost an hour before setting up my tent.

The Wilderness Point primitive campsite at *LL* is just as nice as the Pine Point campsite where I passed my first test, but for different reasons. Both similarly feel secluded in wilderness despite being less than one mile from a paved park road. But while Pine Point sits in an open pine hammock, Wilderness Point sits in a small clearing surrounded by palmetto fields and more densely packed young oaks. Wilderness Point is therefore much smaller and feels cozier than Pine Point. In other words, it feels more like a real backcountry campsite. But it still has the pines and live oaks I relish sleeping beneath. It was also much closer to the sunset-watching hills.

After having previously picked a spot for my tent at Pine Point that was the distance of a long football toss from my picnic table and fire ring, I opted this time for a spot less than 20 feet from the fire. It was nestled so close to palmettos that I felt like I was sleeping beside the low wall of a fort. This time I also folded the front of my tarp near the tent flap door to avoid another soaking from follow-up rains that never came. The kiln-dried firewood stayed dry in the tarp during my hike in, so I unpacked the first two logs and set them on a frame of burnt wood left by the last campers and dug trenches in the sand below to provide tunnels for oxygen.

It was a foregone conclusion that I would not be watching sunset from camp. Shortly before dusk, I headed to a high hill and hoped for more clouds and more colors. I got what I wanted, as the darkening canvas was painted not just blue, white, and orange again, but pink as well, The sunset was just as beautiful as it had been two weeks earlier, and the cold had not yet set in, so I had no problem marveling at the beauty for far longer than I had before.

I even texted sunset photos to my wife and sister. My wife thought they were beautiful. My sister did as well, but she was not yet up to speed on my backpacking fantasy. When I told her I was sleeping in a tent at a state park, she asked if I was okay and assumed my wife had kicked me out of the house and that Chris Farley's van down by the river was booked. (When we talked later that night and I told her about the latest developments at work, she hesitantly suggested that I sounded manic. I am sure her observation was dead-on. But at that moment, I was no longer enraged or despondent.)

I also had not had enough of the appetizer of night hiking that I had tasted at *LL* two weeks earlier, and I decided to make night hiking my main course. The Wilderness Point campsite sits among a gridiron of trails rolling up and over low hills that are wide enough for a car to pass through comfortably, and I knew them all like the back of my hand. After the sunset, I set out to find more deer and anything else that wouldn't bite me. I never found them, but I was comfortable enough at trail junctions to switch my headlamp from red light to off. Even as the chilly wind began nipping at my ears and nose, I trudged deep into the brushy hills away from my campsite, using only stars to illuminate my path.

I returned home for dinner with endorphins still coursing through my veins shortly before 9 p.m.

It was while cooking dinner that I had my biggest failure of the trip. This one almost demoted me to the rank of dumbass scout.

As I mentioned before, the clerks at REI had tried to talk me out of cooking over an open fire with the titanium pot. I had already noticed after my last trip that the fire had left black marks on the pot that could not be washed off. But during dinner this time, I came to fully appreciate the metallurgical characteristics of titanium, and remembered lessons that I should not have forgotten from high school physics.

Titanium is perfect for backcountry crockery. It's lighter and stronger than other metals, so it both reduces weight and saves space. It also transmits heat far better than other metals. This means that you can boil water more quickly than with other metals—and therefore save cooking fuel when you actually listen to your REI clerks and use a stove. It also cools quicker, allowing you to place it back into your backpack quicker and avoid burning yourself so easily.

But like all metals, it expands when subjected to heat, especially when it's submerged in the heat of a large campfire rather than when sitting over the small, focused flame of a small camp stove. This became apparent when I tried to lift my gumbo off the grill of the firepit. My titanium pot had a handle that folded down and in for packing and up and out for use. When I tried to lift the pot off the grill at a less than vertical angle, the heated soft metal bracket that connected the pot to its handle bent unexpectedly, and I spilled half my gumbo into the fire.

I lost half my dinner. And any desire to ever cook dinner on the trail over an open fire again—dumbass mistake.

But all was fine. I still had an extra-large bag of M&Ms that I had not touched while it rained on the hike in, and I figured they would be more constipating than the gumbo anyway. So win-win? I did not go hungry.

I once again had low humidity and a shitload of firewood. I yearned to again be naked, free, and flopping my junk among trees and animals that could not post naked photos of me on Instagram. So I camp-bathed again and stayed naked for as long as I could, until Jack Frost started nipping at my softer parts and I had to put on boxers, the winter hat, gloves, and wool socks. I made less effort with the amateur bear bag but kept it downwind of my tent and fire. I kept the fire going until past 1 a.m., and crawled into my solarium to sleep, having this time brought a nightshade to complement the polyester pants and hooded jacket.

It was here that I learned exactly how wonderful it is to sleep in a sleeping bag with a drawstring. With my gloves preventing the ability to feel with my fingertips, I knew it would disrupt my sleep to have to take my gloves off every time I needed to tighten the opening at the head of my sleeping bag. But I also worried that if I locked the drawstring, I might wake up from a bad dream thinking I had been the victim of a mob hit who had not been finished off before being thrown into the Hudson River in a sack weighed down by cinder blocks. Fortunately, I sleep on my side in the fetal position. I therefore wrapped the drawstring around my gloved hand, pulled the string, and fell asleep wearing the drawstring safely away from my neck. Then each time I was stirred awake by the cold in the middle of the night, I lowered my wrist to my knee and tightened the opening by my head. I also was able to tuck my nicotine vape into the wrist of one of my gloves to avoid fumbling for it in the dark when I needed a hit.

So once again, I slept like a baby beneath the stars, granted, for only about five hours. But in context, this was miraculous. With the tidal wave of depression that had recently hit, I had not slept more than four hours in more than a month in my bed at home. Here, out in the forest in 45-degree cold, with nothing between me and the hard ground but a thin sheet of nylon, a half-inch air cushion, and a smelly airline neck pillow, I had my best night of sleep in more than a month. And for more than fifteen hours, I forgot about my job, my college friends, my mother, and everything else my mind dug up from my subconscious to rob me of peace. I again woke before dawn and enjoyed the rising sun, but this time wondered where the hell the owls were.

When I got out of the tent shortly before it was bright enough to see my shadow, it was cold as fuck. I swear I peed ice cubes. I resisted the urge to cut down the bear bag when my gloves became entangled in rope and moss. The campsite was pretty, but it was far too frozen to stay. I knew the agenda, it was time to find a place to lay down for the sunrise, even if it was too cold to feel my fingers while I tried to pop the top of my iced coffee.

The good news was that the sun was shining brightly, and I had thought to purchase extra tent stakes and bring them with me on the trail. I found a slightly pre-heated patch of trail facing the sun, and this time I lounged on my backpack *under* the poncho instead of on top of it and staked down its corners. In addition to wearing more winter clothing than someone making a summit bid at Everest, I now had a windscreen that retained the warmth from my morning gas. The gas might have ruined breakfast, but the nasty iced coffee tasted worse than my farts. I shivered still, and that morning's sunrise was not as fun as the last one at *LL*, but it was still fun.

I also added in some morning hiking after breakfast, but I quickly realized that losing half my dinner to stupidity had sapped my energy, and I became tired after two miles and returned quickly to camp. I also realized that I had little remaining water. When I became light-headed while pulling my sleeping bag out of my tent, I decided to instead take my camp stool to a sunny rise of the trail near my campsite overlooking the palmetto and longleaf pine. I then rested while sipping my now rationed supply of water. Camp Fail Number 2, check.

My energy eventually returned, and I had no problem breaking camp and packing my gear for the two-mile jaunt out. I also was able to spend more time relaxing on the stool atop the picnic table while the sun rose high enough to warm the trail for the hike out. I avoided the temptation to use paved roads for a shortcut back to my car, and the two-mile hike out ended up being easy. My car was parked this time at Dixie Lake, so I did not have to drive anywhere for the relaxing lakeside contemplation before driving home. I met a nice park ranger who responded to my inquiry about the nearest water fountain by filling half my empty Nalgene bottle with water from her own bottle. She could not have been nicer, and I have yet to meet a park ranger who was any less friendly. I had passed my final solo backpacking exam, even if I had to settle for a B-minus.

When I returned home that Saturday afternoon, I still had one more entire day to relax before attempting to return to work. But the depression and anxiety returned almost immediately. The Gators basketball team beat Missouri that night, and although I enjoyed watching the game, I still ranted and raged about work, friends, and my mother during commercial breaks. I then slept less than three hours and woke up again at 5 a.m. A relaxing Sunday with my family broke the pattern only sporadically. The only way I could relieve my mind from despair was thinking about my latest trip to *LL*, fantasizing about the next trip, and rehearsing what I would discuss with my therapist at my next appointment. I also had to figure out what I was going to tell my boss if I did not feel better by the next morning.

I intended to return to working from home that Monday, but after another sleepless night and another rough morning, it just wasn't going to happen. I texted my team that I could not work again but would still speak with my boss as soon as he wanted to talk and invited him to call me on my cell phone. I was now losing the ability to think rationally. I knew I needed more time to get myself back together.

I was still noticeably rattled when my boss called to figure out our next steps. I remember little about the call, except that I was honest and did not know what to do. He understood my desperate mental state, and one or both of us suggested that I take that week off and that we talk again that Friday to decide how to proceed. I do recall that his greatest concern was my well-being, and he asked me to figure out what I needed to get better. I also remember him saying that if I needed to resign, that would be all right. The word "sabbatical" also came up. I hung up the phone in shame at the end of our conversation.

I avoided television during working hours that week to avoid feeling like a deadbeat piece of shit—I was not going to conform to the stereotype and sit around eating bonbons and gain back all the weight I had fought so hard to lose. I continued walking five miles a day around my neighborhood in the dorky Tevas and socks, and I continued reading another history tome for several hours a day. I was still depressed and still wretched every time I thought about having to deal with case managers, and I suspected I was finally reaching the breaking point from years of work-related stress.

I also kept mulling over the sabbatical that was mentioned during my call with my boss. I began realizing that I needed a complete break from work, and I knew my wife and I had sufficient savings that we could afford a few months without income from me if I watched my spending. So after meeting with my therapist, I began formulating a plan to get better. The only questions were how long of a break I needed and whether my boss would go for it.

When I spoke with my boss that Friday, we agreed that I would take an indefinite unpaid sabbatical. I am sure this put him in a difficult position, but I gratefully accepted his willingness to allow me the time to get better and promised to return to work as soon as I could. I told him that I suspected I would need at least two months, maybe longer if I did not improve as quickly as I hoped. He told me that my health was all that mattered and that we would figure it all out once I got better. I told my assistants as soon as I got off the phone with my boss, thanked them and apologized for the problems I was causing them, and promised to keep them updated as I made progress. I then broke free for the near future from the stresses of practicing law.

But that did not happen before I had my worst panic attack to date. The night before I called my boss to propose my sabbatical, I made the foolish mistake of asking my wife to check my bank account to see if I had received my latest paycheck, which was due that week, although probably not until the next day anyway. I was also worried about the possibility that my boss might not agree to the sabbatical and that he may be growing tired of my time away from work.

I have an extremely analytical mind that instnctively assesses litigation and life-decisions like a field general managing a major offensive through the fog of war. Before making even minor strategic decisions, whether for work or family, my mind takes in all the facts and identifies the panoply of possible outcomes of different courses of action. This has always helped me in litigation by allowing me to identify what is really important in a given case and to forecast the potential benefits and risks of any strategic decision, even when the stakes are high and the future is uncertain. But when I am depressed, I focus on worst-case scenarios, and my mind dwells on the most apocalyptic outcome.

So when my wife told me around 8:00 the night before I had my Friday call with my boss that I had not yet received my latest paycheck, I immediately jumped to the conclusion that my boss had withheld my paycheck because he intended to fire me. In fairness, I acknowledged throughout the night that the chances of that happening were probably extremely low. But if it *did* happen, I was truly fucked because I had not prepared for that risk. Although I had been seeing my therapist by then for three weeks, I had not yet asked for a "doctor's note" to miss work or provided one to my boss. I had no contemporaneous proof that I was unable to work because of an impairment to my mental health and had not even asked for one yet.

My mind never stops there. After all, I had a family to support, and if I was fired, I presumed it would be difficult to get another job practicing law. I thought about what I could do to persuade my boss to reverse the hypothetical and outlandishly unlikely decision to terminate me, knowing that he was as skilled a litigator and tactician as me. I reasoned in my desperate mania that if my boss chose to now believe that I was missing work without justification and to terminate me immediately, I would have no proof to present in interviews with potential future employers that he had acted unfairly. (Not that I would ever want to tell them about my mental health problems anyway.) Sure, I could get the proof I needed soon, but I would not have it before the termination occurred.

And I jumped to the conclusion that this might have already happened.

And I panicked. As best I can recall, I ranted again incoherently at breakneck speed for hours despite again being sober (at least for the first few hours), and I again resisted all attempts by my wife to convince me that I was not going to be fired. (This also again happened on my patio, and I suspect my poor neighbors turned up their televisions to avoid hearing the latest psychotic rants from the neighbor who liked to sleep in his backyard.) We were back to running around in circles, forcing my wife to watch the same bad movie over and over for hours on end without being able to change the channel. It was just like Christmas Eve, except this time, I got worse as the night wore on.

I now realized that I was not just depressed, I was hopeless and paranoid. The scariest part was that I knew what I was doing and was trying all I could to stop it from happening. I thought about the two trips to *LL* and the sunrises and sunsets. I thought about the recent advice from my therapist, and how lucky I was to have a supportive wife, a loving daughter, a boss who allowed me time to figure out my problems, and a home in a neighborhood where I could rant outside under the stars. I even said aloud repeatedly how there was little chance I would be fired and that I would know for sure the next day. But I could not stop panicking. My mind was deliberately working against me, projecting a horror film of the worst-case scenario for my life on the movie screen inside my brain. I could not even catch my breath, let alone calm down.

I also knew I needed to get some sleep, otherwise I would not be able to talk to my boss the next day and would have to postpone and prolong the torture of not knowing through another weekend. That could not happen, the pain had to end. I absolutely *must* sleep. But I could not slow my panicking mind down enough to even sit still; I was miles away from being tired as midnight approached.

I therefore went back to what I knew was most likely to work. I pulled a chaise lounge out to the darkest part of my patio and I pulled out my sleeping bag. I had my wife help close all the blinds, not to keep light outside from getting in, but to keep any light inside the house from sneaking outside to me. It was time to try sleeping under the stars without a tent. I uncorked a bottle of wine, Champagne left over from New Year's Eve, and I got the next bottle ready in case I needed that one as well. I drank the first glass quickly, and within five minutes I was able to stop talking for the first time in hours.

I kept the bottle outside with me and slowly drank a second glass, and my analytical mind charted my transition to intoxication like play-by-play commentators calling a baseball game. Within 30 minutes of opening the bottle, my mind transformed from panicking lunatic to nerdy scientist, then to a dark stand-up comedian. I still wallowed in apocalyptic negativity, but now it was becoming funny in a Coen Brothers/ Tarantino kind of way. I began laughing at the corner I had backed myself into. The humor of it all calmed my nerves, and I slowly became tired. I had tricked myself into sleeping this way in the old days.

I finished the first bottle of wine, went inside, opened the next bottle, poured another glass, and took it outside and set it beside the chaise lounge. I unzipped the sleeping bag and put my ankles inside, lowered the back of the chair enough to reduce the heartburn but still drink, and stared at the stars. Slowly I stopped thinking. I had no idea what time it was, but at least my wife was in bed. I was exhausted enough to believe she might be sleeping, and I whispered apologies to her silently.

The nearly full first glass from the second bottle of wine was sitting beside me when I woke up as usual at 5:00 a.m. I did not drink beyond memory—I have never done so except once during a trip to Mardi Gras my freshman year of college—and I clearly remembered everything that had happened the night before, including the pain and exhaustion I saw painted on my wife's face for all those hours.

I also knew that I would be talking to my boss in a few hours, and I started rehearsing what I would say for the call. I was not going to let this continue. I was going to pull myself together and talk to my boss, no matter how much I feared what he would say. As I had many times when pulling myself together before hearings after panic attacks, I focused on the mission, prepared for the challenge, and compartmentalized everything else to be revisited after the conversation occurred. Maybe it's my background in theater. When the curtain opens, you must go out on stage and perform, no matter what is going on in your head. My mind began playing Nirvana's "On a Plain" instinctively.

Of course, I knew I was still a misplaced thought or word away from revving up again to 100 miles an hour. But I was exhausted, and I was still just intoxicated enough to not begin ranting again. So I took extra hits from my nicotine vape to make sure I kept my wits about me until my wife came to check on me in a few hours. Then I could recalibrate and prepare for the negotiation.

I was also soaking wet. It had been a humid night, and my sleeping bag was a soppy sponge inside and out, as were my skin, hair, and clothes. I cannot remember if I was too cold or too warm. But I still had the stars for at least another hour. I made the best of a tough situation and prepared for the big call, at which I ultimately got permission to take the sabbatical I needed. I was not fired after all. Shocker, I had become all riled up for nothing. I mentioned nothing about my fears of being fired during the call with my boss.

I also decided to immediately contact a psychiatrist and get back on meds.

As soon as I got off the phone with my boss and confirmed that I could take a sabbatical, I immediately felt better and clear-headed. I also committed myself completely to doing whatever it took to get better and to making the long road ahead as comfortable as I could for my wife and daughter. After all, they had no idea what was coming, but I did, and I knew how to protect them. I had been there before.

It went without saying that I would not overeat or watch television or otherwise fuck off during weekdays. I would spend all weekday working hours sober and either reading, writing, going to therapy, hiking, exercising, or doing chores to relieve the burden on my wife (I had never been much use in that department before). I barely drank anymore anyway because of the impact alcohol had made on my prior efforts to lose weight, so the only tricky part I anticipated was staying focused on productive activities.

As I mentioned before, I also quickly booked an appointment with a psychiatrist for as soon as possible, which turned out to be almost two weeks later. When I had started therapy several weeks earlier, I did not want to return to meds because I felt that I had gotten better before only by changing unhealthy behaviors. It's not that I was against antidepressants, I knew that some people absolutely need them. But I was afraid to rely upon them, especially given that I was an irresponsible shit when I last took them in the late 1990s and missed doses routinely. I now realized that I *was* now one of those people who needed antidepressants, and I needed to start taking them immediately. I knew that most need at least a month or two to start taking effect, and they often need to be adjusted with new meds. This would also happen to me shortly with intense impact on my life. So the clock was ticking. I also knew that meds could help me sleep.

I also decided to cut off contact with everyone other than my wife, daughter, sister, and physicians for the near future, and I needed to limit my contact with my sister. It was not that she was a bad influence. Quite to the contrary, I was thrilled that we had recently reconnected after an eight-year hiatus caused by a fight. But she had suffered enough the last time depression had knocked me out of orbit, and I was not going to put her or my brother-in-law through any of that again. Besides, she was several states away, and it's just too hard to hear someone you love crying or raging on the other end of a phone line without being able to see them in person the next day to know they are okay. I decided I would update her about my progress but spare her from the gory details of any challenging times.

I would obviously also avoid all contact with my parents for the time being and filter any communications through my wife. I knew this wouldn't be hard to do because I had been doing that for years already.

I also reminded myself that I would recover and had advantages that most people suffering with depression and anxiety do not have. I had a loving, supportive wife and a loving daughter who never significantly misbehaves. I had a good therapist and the financial resources to afford her, and I would soon have a good psychiatrist. I had a supportive employer who was giving me the space I needed to get well, and I knew just how rare that is.

Most importantly, I had the critical experience of having gone through it all before and came out vastly improved. It was not just that my prior experience gave me hope. I knew what to look for, good and bad. I knew the innocuous baby steps forward that are often major breakthroughs that most people cannot appreciate. I also knew the bad habits or minor signs that could lead to crisis and suicidal ideation, and I knew how to neutralize them if I had the self-control to do so. I also knew that the right medications would give me that self-control and would allow me to extinguish fires before they burned down the entire forest.

Knowing that my mind would obsess about the worst-case scenarios, I acknowledged what was at stake. If I ever became suicidal, it would ruin my daughter's life and at best, irrevocably harm my wife. I had spent my entire life afraid that I would pass on my illness to my daughter through the bloodstream, and I realized that allowing her to ever see me in such a desperate state could condemn her to a similar future. But I also knew from my sister's experience that she could equally suffer from inattention. I knew that because she loves me, keeping her in the dark could also cause her to suffer unnecessarily. I planned the best ways to shield her from the rough stuff, but also tell her when I'm okay and answer any of her questions in the most gentle but honest way possible.

I also knew, even in my depressed state, that I had a special opportunity. I had always known that I would one day tell my daughter about what happened in 1999, if for no other reason than to allow her to understand problems she may face long after my wife and I are gone. I also knew that if I could get well after becoming seriously mentally ill, I would give her the hope of knowing that everything would be fine if indeed she ever suffered as I was suffering now. I could save her by showing her the path that I already knew how to follow. And I was only afforded this opportunity because of my illness. As you might imagine, this gave me hope and an inspiring reason to do all I could to get well as soon as possible.

I also decided that I would continue backpacking. It's certainly true that backpacking can be life-threatening to people with a history of suicidal depression, and I did not make this decision without thorough consideration. I discussed it with my wife and therapist and made sure they both felt comfortable with me continuing. I also let them know that I did not intend to take any risks pressing myself beyond my limits or testing those limits too severely. I am not a thrill junkie, and I did not intend to become one now.

But I knew that something profound was happening to me in the forest. I could already notice changes that *had* to be healthy. My strange ability to sleep outdoors has already been well-documented. I had also somehow avoided being frightened by solitude and darkness, even though I had feared the dark and the quiet my entire life. If backpacking truly was unhealthy, why did I only find relief from anxiety while doing it? The physical exertion also helped my self-esteem, as my body was now becoming fit. For the first time, I was starting to see the outline of abdominal muscles, and I could even see back muscles emerging from what had been gallons of back flab less than nine months earlier.

I also knew that my secret weapon against depression was my never resting, unquiet, fantasizing mind. Through my toughest times at the big national law firm, I was able to retain hope by planning trips to football games and Las Vegas, which distracted me from obsessing about the negative events of my life. By focusing on learning about Florida's geography and natural history and planning backpacking trips, I might just be able to distract my mind from obsessing about the bad things happening to me now until medications helped change my brain chemistry.

Besides, I now had an open calendar and all the time I needed to plan my next adventures.

Lake Kissimmee State Park, March 30, 2024.

Overlook of Tiger Creek, at Tiger Creek Preserve, February 1, 2024.

Tricia's Peak, Tiger Creek Preserve, February 1, 2024.

CHAPTER SIX

Falling in Love with My Home

G| will forever be fascinated by Florida's geological history. The sands I hike on and that my home is built upon have not been here forever. They were part of the mountain range we now call the Appalachians that was formed between 490 and 250 million years ago, when two ancient supercontinents called Laurentia and Gondwana collided to form the supercontinent of Pangea.[5] The Appalachians were part of a continuous 6,000-kilometer chain of mountains that stretched from the Arctic to the Pacific Oceans, remnants of which can be found across the world today.[6] At that time, the land that eventually became Florida was hundreds of miles from any ocean, and the Appalachians may have been as many as 8,000 meters high—nearly as tall as Mount Everest is today.[7]

Beginning about 200 million years ago, Pangea began splitting apart, and a rift that eventually filled with water and became the Atlantic Ocean began widening between what eventually became the southeastern coast of the United States and the northwestern coast of Africa.[8] As the continents drifted further apart, the Appalachian Mountains eroded to the 2,000-meter stubs they are today.[9] The finest of quartz sentiments from what had previously been those mountains were transported by rivers and ocean currents to the portions of Florida that I hike on today.[10]

Before all those sediments arrived, little of Florida was actual dry land. When the meteor that killed the non-avian dinosaurs 65.5 million years ago struck a shallow sea near where the Yucatan Peninsula now lies, Florida was beneath the ocean.[11] At that time, the Florida Platform was being built up slowly from the ocean floor by a number of processes, including the piling up of billions of tiny carcasses of organisms that lived and died before the dinosaurs last walked the earth.[12] Eventually the land rose close enough to the surface to allow eroding sands from the Appalachian Mountains to rise above the water and form islands that were exposed, submerged, and then exposed and submerged again and again above and beneath salty seas between ice ages over millions of years. That's why you can find fossilized teeth of ancient megalodons in Central Florida not far from skeletons of mammoths and saber-toothed cats.[13]

That is also why *LL* sits on hilly land that rises just miles west of where I live, and forms part of a ridge of sandy hills that stretches south almost all the way to Lake Okeechobee,[14] creating a beautiful rolling ocean of pine, oak, and palmetto that is among the most beautiful places I've ever seen. Much of it is now being bulldozed into subdivisions, strip malls, and toll roads, and much more will be destroyed in the coming decades. But many of those places are still quite natural, and many of the best parts are accessible only by winding trails too narrow for cars or ATVs or even horses. Some are even too far from paved roads to hear the murmur of cars or the ear-splitting grunge they often emit after midnight when driven by people like me. A precious few of those places are rarely even passed over by airliners.

Through the trail guides I purchased from REI in December, I began finding many of these places shortly after I began my sabbatical. I was not yet ready to backpack there. I first needed to restore my senses and obtain the advice of a psychiatrist as to what medication would help me deal with my demons. But nothing prevented me from hiking. And if I was going to start solo backpacking, I needed to start carrying at least a partially loaded backpack longer distances on trails I had not yet hiked.

I had already been planning my first *real* backpacking trip beyond *LL* (more on that shortly), but while I waited for my appointment with the psychiatrist, I searched out trails less than two-hours' drive away where I could carry the same partial 20-pound load as I had while studying for the final exam at *LL*. Because of how much I revered *LL*, I focused on the hills of the Lake Wales Ridge south of where I live, using the books I bought when I first started backpacking. And I found a piece of heaven on earth.

Tiger Creek Preserve is a wonderland of hikers only trails managed by The Nature Conservancy with unfortunately no camping allowed. *LL* seems like Central Park compared to the isolation of Tiger Creek Preserve. Its winding, well-blazed paths meander through palmetto fields of longleaf pine, dense hammocks of bromeliad-covered oaks that barely rise above your head, sandy fields that call to mind southwestern desert oases, marshes overlooked by sandhills, and creeks banked with cabbage palm. It is also nearly devoid of people (other than extremely friendly land managers). This is also the only place I have been in Florida where I have never heard a car or seen a plane, and I've now been there four times.

Tiger Creek Preserve also has hills—its nearly twelve miles of connected trails roll over hills almost as high as those at *LL*, but with 360-degree panoramic views of nothing but pine, prairie, palmetto, and water. The best example is Tricia's Peak, where a covered pair of benches honoring one of the preserve's managers sits atop one of the highest pine ridges in the preserve. While enjoying a respite from a sunny hike, you see nothing in all directions but natural beauty and hear nothing but the breeze and the beating of your heart. This is bar none my favorite place to have lunch anywhere in Florida. A different stretch of the trail rises almost twenty feet above the blackwater Tiger Creek itself, a majestic setting where you expect to see 19th century settlers pass by on the trail. The benches and blazes are as well-maintained as I have seen anywhere in Florida, even the Florida National Scenic Trail.

On my first trip, I took extra water and extra weight, but I hardly noticed when the app on my phone told me that I had gone more than 11 miles. I would have finer experiences backpacking in the coming weeks, but not many.

It was around this time that I also decided to break a big rule about social media. I have long looked down on people who post photos of their dinners on Facebook, and I had only begrudgingly obtained a Facebook account several years earlier when guilt tripped while serving as President of my Gator Club by our Communications VP for not reposting club events. I was also paranoid about the partners at that big national law firm knowing too much about my personal life or my road trips to Gator games. Thus, I have never posted original content on my Facebook page. I also have very few Facebook friends, as I never accept "friend" requests from family members other than my sister and brother-in-law, or even *real friends* with whom I work, as I never wanted to have to explain to a judgmental partner why I didn't want to be social media "friends."

But after passing my final exam at *LL*, I knew I would be doing more solo backpacking trips, I knew they were special to me, and I knew I wanted to document and learn from them. I did not think at the time that I would ever write a book about them. But I didn't want my only documentation of those trips to be photos on my phone and whatever I could remember about where I was and what I saw when I took them.

Still, I did not want to post anything about my backpacking trips on my Facebook page, especially after I saw the glazed disinterest in the eyes of the few neighbors I told about hiking and my backpacking dream. Even the teacher of Man Class from Colorado, who had camped with his wife in national forests before they moved to Florida, started staring at his phone the minute I mentioned hiking or camping and quickly changed the subject. Perhaps I was just overly sensitive because of my mental health issues, but I did not want people judging me or labeling me a bragging hippie if I indiscriminately broadcast the experiences that mattered so much to me on social media to people who didn't care. But I *had* to write about them, even if my only audience was myself. And with the technological IQ of a dyslexic cave man, I could not think of any other straightforward way to document my experiences with photographs and commentary other than by using the Facebook machine on the magic phone with a camera.

So after discussing my needs with my much more tech-savvy wife, we produced a solution. I would create a private Facebook group, and I would invite only people who I thought might care about my backpacking adventures to join. Of course, because I had never posted on the Big FB before and barely knew how to accept a friend request, I had to let my wife set up the group and invite me to join. She also had to teach me how to post. I called it *My Secret World*, and I have regretted ever since being unable to come up with a better name that doesn't sound like a short story aimed at pre-pubescent girls.

As a testament to my sensitivity at the time, I even posted the following mission statement right before I created my first posts documenting the two nights at *LL*:

> This Facebook page is a creative solution to a unique problem. I recently lost more than one-third of my weight through diet and exercise, and my priorities have shifted from

seeing how much weight I can lose to engaging in activities that have been foreclosed to me for decades. Many of these have drawn me back outdoors and to activities lost to me since adolescence.

One of those activities is backpacking—my first backpacking trip since the 1990s triggered the creation of this page. I have a strong desire to document my new adventures, and Facebook is obviously perfect for that.

But I have two problems. First, I have no desire to publicize what I'm doing. I'm creating this page only to document and learn from my experiences, not to brag about them to Facebook friends. That is why I'm not posting about these experiences on an existing Facebook page.

Also, I worry that if I share what I've been doing with the rest of the world, most won't get it. I am backpacking, not camping, and the distinction matters. Backpacking involves not just camping, but carrying into nature only what you can carry on your back and enjoying nature without portable stereos and iPads or the creature comforts of civilization. For most, camping seems to involve taking into nature all that can fit into a vehicle and enjoying the comforts of home in an outdoor parking lot. To me, this ignores nature and spoils any true value that might be had.

I'm therefore reluctant to share my experiences with people who won't understand what I'm doing or why or what is so special about them. The sad reality is that most with whom I've shared my forays into nature dismiss the value of the outdoors. That is why the events displayed here are *My Secret World*—It is not secret because I am hiding it, but because people can't see its value even though it is visible to all.

After I later learned how to post videos, I added the following postscript, "One more note: This page contains some videos that I sent to my wife to share my experiences and let her know I'm happy and safe. Out of context, they may sound like douchey brag posts, and I often sound like a gay DJ on an easy listening radio station (I'm usually tired when I shoot them). But these weren't taken for public consumption, and the douchey tone is accidental."

It was shortly after visiting nirvana at Tiger Creek Preserve that I finally met with my psychiatrist. It went well, and he unsurprisingly confirmed that I had major problems with anxiety and prescribed a cheaper over-the-counter version of Prozac. I would later learn that he diagnosed me with *intermittent explosive disorder*, an impairment through which sufferers overreact to minor conflicts and rage in ways that are not understood by even friends and family. The irony of the first three letters being a military acronym for the homemade landmines that killed so many American servicemen in Iraq was not lost on me and was fitting; it certainly helped explain my recent behavior. My psychiatrist also warned that the Prozac may not take effect for more than a month, and I may never notice any change at all. I thanked him, got the prescription, and prepared to begin taking medication again.

But to avoid any risk of unexpected side effects while in a place where I might not be able to cope safely, I decided to wait to begin taking the meds until after I returned from my first *real* backpacking trip a few days after meeting with my psychiatrist. There was never any question about where I would do my first backpacking trip outside *LL*.

From the first time I saw it in one of my trail guides, I knew the Prairie Loop at Kissimmee Prairie Preserve State Park would be perfect for my first true backpacking trip. Set among 54,000 acres not far off the Florida Turnpike about two hours southeast of my home, Kissimmee Prairie Preserve is Florida's only certified star watching dark sky park because of its distance from any metropolitan areas that could drown out the night sky in city lights. Its 4.6-mile Prairie Loop is also easy, and although I suspected I could do longer distances, I preferred to avoid taking chances attempting to navigate an unknown trail for the first time with 40 pounds on my back. Its primitive campsite, nestled in a palm and live oak hammock surrounded by endless flat palmetto prairie, is also two miles west of the only small portion of the park lit at night by RVs and parking lot campers.

Even better, I booked the primitive campsite the night before a new moon when the stars would be brightest. And because I chose to go on a Thursday rather than the weekend of the new moon which was sure to be the busiest of the month, I was the only one at the campsite.

To prepare for this first *real* backpacking adventure, I made upgrades to my gear. First and most importantly, I finally purchased a small camp stove and new titanium crockery. The stove was a Soto Amicus, a tiny burner with four steel arms that fold out with a push-button igniter that screws into the top of a small isobutane/propane fuel canister, and which folds down to the size of a human thumb. The new titanium crockery was a two-pot set that could be carried in a small bag, and the inner circumference of each pot is just large enough to snugly hold the fuel canister. I therefore would not have to worry about an IED rattling around inside my backpack while I jostled it down the trail. I also threw in a small titanium coffee mug.

For food, I finally listened to Professor Helmuth. I visited the aisle at REI with the fancy freeze-dried dinners and purchased one meal each from three different brands to determine which I preferred in coming trips (I now prefer Peak). I skipped the breakfast aisle and as instructed by Professor H., instead bought single-serving packets of oatmeal from the grocery store and took two packets on the trail. I reconnected with instant coffee and similarly bought single-serve packets from the grocery store. I went with Death Wish, which claims on the box to have been invented by NASA for astronauts and has 300 milligrams of caffeine in each eight-ounce cup. It tastes as good as it sounds, but it cut the time I required to break camp in half.

By bringing the camp stove, I no longer had to rely on fire to cook, so I was finally able to reduce my kiln-dried wood weight, but still being an amateur, I only reduced it from 15 pounds to 7 pounds. It would take a while before I figured out what I was doing. I also brought more water after the near problem I had during my final exam at *LL*.

The trip was a blast, although in retrospect, I don't think I remember how great it was because of how much fun I had on subsequent trips. The arrival to the park is notable in how far you must drive after reaching the park's entrance to see a human—more than 20 minutes down dusty, straight roads surrounded by almost nothing but palmetto. I had no problem finding the trailhead, where I immediately began shooting photos for my next *Secret World* post. I arrived somewhat late in the afternoon, but I had no problem getting to the campsite quickly during the largely shadeless 2.1-mile hike in. It more than exceeded my expectations.

The Prairie Loop campsite is three sites in one. One has a convenient shelter large enough for a tent when it rains. Nice as it was, I immediately rejected that site because the tree cover was too dense to see stars. Another site further down the trail similarly had too much tree cover. But the last site behind a water pump backed up to the prairie and sat slightly higher than the sea of palmetto below. On the downside, there was a powerline in the distance, but the views for the stars were unobstructed. Best of all, it faced east, so I knew I'd have a first-class bedroom from which to watch the sunrise.

I quickly set up my tent and, having a restless mind, decided to immediately do some exploring. The sunset was right around the corner, and there were enough clouds to make it a special one. I hiked down a long wide trail transecting the Prairie Loop near my camp. I was initially worried about wet conditions and even alligators (I had seen alligators uncomfortably close to the trail at Paynes Prairie State Park near Gainesville earlier that year when hiking with my family), but the trail was bone dry, and I quickly realized I had nothing to fear. I hiked down two miles before turning around, and only chose to not go further because the sun was beginning to dip low on the horizon.

I returned to camp shortly before dusk, and I knew now was no time to eat. It was time to find my lounge chair for premium star watching. I took out my bug wipes, lathered up, and took my backpack, camp stool, and poncho a few hundred yards past my camp down the Prairie Loop. I spread out my poncho on a wide part of the trail that I decided would be safe enough to see any creepy critters coming, and I waited for the stars to arrive while seeing the most gorgeous sunset of my life.

The stars did not disappoint, although an approaching cloud bank did not bode well for stargazing from bed. You have no idea how many stars are out there when you live anywhere near a city or suburb. There are literally hundreds visible on a cloudless night of a new moon. I spent two hours after dark counting stars and drawing my own constellations with my imagination. During Man Class, my neighbor had used an app to determine that the band of three stars that I thought was part of *some dipper* is actually Orion's belt. That night, I saw the whole archer with flexed bow and taut arrow.

Many twinkled, others glistened. The worshipper of sunrises and sunsets now became infatuated with stars, too.

My stomach began rumbling around the time clouds rolled across half the sky, and I knew it was time to see if I could make dinner for the first time with the burner-bomb contraption without blowing up the campsite. I had to scare an opossum from the front of my campsite when I returned (those suckers are not scared of anything), but dinner was easy and there were no third-degree burns. The only mistake I made was placing the freeze-dried meal into the pot of boiling water, rather than pouring the water into the sealable packet. This caused me to bite into the silver packet used to keep the food . . . well, whatever that packet does, and required unnecessary dish washing. That was not a problem this time because of the nearby water pump, although I did dump the dirty water a few hundred feet down the trail to avoid attracting hungry mammals.

The fire, public nudity, and yuppie bath were all a joy as usual, although I finally realized that I didn't need to bring so much wood when the three-hour fire lasted longer than desired. I finally was legitimately sleepy when I went into the tent, and after putting in ear plugs when fearing that the opossum had returned to harass me from the bushes near my tent, I fell asleep gently and quickly.

That morning was the first time I came to truly learn why I backpack. I woke up a half-hour before sunrise with my rain cover retracted. What I saw outside my tent blew me away with its beauty. The early rays of dawn were slowly creeping over the horizon and glistening off the tops of the palms and live oaks. A low bank of fog sat feet off the prairie

View from inside my tent at dawn at Kissimmee Prairie Preserve State Park, February 9, 2024.

Breakfast at campsite at dawn at Kissimmee Prairie Preserve State Park, February 9, 2024.

among the palmetto while nearby birds began announcing the morning. I took the first of what would become many videos in easy listening DJ voice and sent them to my wife. I then took another 360-panorama video right after stepping out of my tent and watering the palmettos. By then, the sunbeams had reached the wide ropes of moss hanging from the live oaks a few paces down the hammock beach from my tent. I walked there slowly and passed my hands through the moss like a hippie yoga master. This was going to be a nice breakfast.

After cooking up my gut cleaner coffee and throwing a few M&Ms from my trail mix into my bowl of oatmeal, I took them back beside my tent and had a long, hot breakfast in a scene that, but for the powerline in the distance, was as special as Tricia's Peak. This was not a place to be abandoned, so with no need to rush and only a 2.5-mile hike out with less weight, I enjoyed a relaxing morning at camp. I'd been through a lot lately; this was a refreshing way to wake up. It also helped restore my faith that things would get better.

The hike out was nothing special—the one drawback of Kissimmee Prairie Preserve is the relative monotony of prairie without forest—yet the hike was easy. I briefly considered turning left and away from the trail at the intersection with the old Military Road (which I later learned was my first experience hiking the Florida National Scenic Trail), and after seeing overgrown brush and an outline that looked too much like a gator, I turned around and sheepishly began the quick walk back to my car. The sunny morning had become breezy, and so was the hike out. I was no longer testing solo backpacking, I was now officially doing it, and I was hooked.

Before I reached Kissimmee Prairie Preserve State Park, I did have another panic attack. But it resulted in one of those small steps forward that I knew was an early milestone.

I had scheduled a pre-colonoscopy the morning of my trip, and although I arrived early for my appointment, I expected a wait. I should have taken it as a bad sign when they asked to run my credit card before the appointment rather than after I had seen the masseuse. The waiting room was full, and I had a bad feeling that the wait would be longer than usual.

It was. Under even normal circumstances (at least before the Prozac started kicking in), I have debilitating impatience. It is the first thing I reported to both my therapist and my psychiatrist when I first met with them. That problem had been aggravated by my latest problems, and the gastroenterologist's office was not an ideal place to cope with impatience. I quickly realized that the office was understaffed. Even though I was second on the waiting list, none of the patients in the waiting room had been called 45 minutes after I arrived, and the other patients were also getting restless.

As my blood began to boil and my muscles began to tighten, I tried to calm myself by reading. But a woman around my mother's age sitting across from me was on the phone, and despite being the only one talking, she was talking loudly. Loudly enough to not need the phone to be heard by the person on the other end of the line miles away. And she was complaining—bitching about the same kinds of things my mother bitches about. Neighbors and people who drive like jerks. Lazy people who don't work for a living. The regular Reagan-era vitriol.

After an hour, I could no longer take it. I walked to the front desk and told the receptionist that I could no longer wait and would have to reschedule. She told me that would be fine, but they could not refund my payment.

At this point I paused. There was obviously a chance I would detonate right there in front of her desk. But with everything else going on in my life, I instead felt like I was about to burst into an uncontrollable fit of tears, right there in front of a room full of people about to deal with a different kind of pain in the ass. My mind raced as it panicked about what to do. Should I just walk out and abandon the payment?

At any time in the past, I would have gotten aggressive and told the receptionist that it's ridiculous that they didn't wait until after I received medical care to charge me, that I'll dispute the charge with my credit card company if needed, et cetera. But I knew this would cause me shame by making me look like a jerk. This time, I tried a new course of action.

In the calmest voice I could muster, I told the receptionist, "I apologize, but I just started treatment for depression and severe anxiety. I was prescribed medication by my psychiatrist earlier this week, but I have not yet started taking it. I understand the reason for the wait, but I'm starting to feel extremely anxious, and I'm worried about what I'll do if I can't get out of here soon. Is there any way I can have my payment refunded and reschedule my appointment for some time later when I feel better?"

I expected nothing but a cold no. I'd never had the courage to tell anyone I'd met in the prior 15 years about my mental health problems, much less a stranger. I never expected anyone to understand or care. The last place I expected to receive sympathy was the waiting room of a doctor's office—I would have expected more humanity from the DMV. But instead, the receptionist whispered that she would ask her manager about the refund.

One minute later she returned and told me that my payment would be refunded and that she hoped I would feel better soon. I walked directly out of the waiting room without looking at the rude lady on the phone, and I held back the tears just long enough to get past the front door of the office. I immediately started taking deep drags from my nicotine vape while trying to slow down my heart rate and wiping the waterworks from my face. It was theoretically time to go to Kissimmee Prairie Preserve and I had my backpack ready in my car, but I knew better than to drive in such a condition. I leaned against the hood of my car and stared at the sky away from passing pedestrians and took deep breaths for 15 minutes, contemplating what had just happened.

For the first time in my life, I had trusted a stranger enough to tell them about my mental illness and to ask for sympathy and understanding. To my surprise, that stranger did not judge me and instead helped me. And for the first time, I had dealt with a panic attack in a public place in a way that did not make me look and feel like an asshole. Scary as the experience was, I knew this was a major step toward getting better.

CHAPTER SEVEN

Valentine's Day in the Forest

I knew after I passed the first test at *LL* on the first weekend in January (before I even thought about taking a sabbatical) that I would try to do at least a few backpacking trips in February and possibly early March. That is, if I could find available reservations at primitive campsites along trails of at least five or six miles at nearby state parks. Even after I completed my first *real* backpacking trip to Kissimmee Prairie Preserve State Park on February 9th, I did not expect to do more than a couple more trips because of family and work commitments. We had a spring break trip to Arizona coming in the second week of March, two weekends after my wife had a college reunion. I was not sure I'd be doing any trips in March before the spring break trip because of time constraints, and I expected it to be too hot to backpack after we returned. I also doubted that I would have the physical stamina to do weekly trips in February.

But after I returned from Kissimmee Prairie Preserve, I felt stronger and more confident. What's more, because of my sabbatical, I was no longer restricted to backpacking on weekends but could instead take trips mid-week when campsites were less likely to be reserved. This was especially fortuitous for a three-day/two-night trip that I hoped to be strong enough to do and that I anticipated to be the climax of my first backpacking season. Because of my sleep and sweat issues, I preferred to do trips during colder weather, anticipating that I'd avoid pressing my luck too far with the sleep gods and hoping to avoid my first sleepless night on the trail.

Each week in February, a new *El Niño*-induced weather wave seemed to roll in right in the middle of the week, during the time my wife and daughter were least available because of school and work. I was therefore afforded the luxury of identifying a new trail for backpacking each week, watching the weekly weather forecast, and reserving campsites as soon as I knew the best days to go. This allowed me to scout weather forecasts like a surfer watching approaching fronts for perfect swells.

As it turned out, although I did not originally envision doing so, I took weekly backpacking trips during each of the four weeks in February, such that by the end of the month, I had taken six inexpensive fantasy vacations in the first two months of the year, at exactly the time when I could really use the distraction from otherwise crippling depression while I waited for the Prozac to kick in. At a time when my obsessively negative mind was trying its best to make me miserable, I had plenty of life-changing adventures to distract myself and a much more recent collection of good memories to think about instead.

As much as I might have liked to head immediately after my first *true* backpacking trip to my fantasy two-nighter, I knew I was not yet ready and needed to prepare for longer distances with full loads on my back, particularly on hikes with more weight during warmer afternoons. Because I was confining my gaze at the time to state parks, my nearby options with sufficient trail distance were limited. I considered Wekiwa Springs, but it was too familiar (I'd already hiked there more than 40 times over the past several years), and I also worried about bears that I had seen while hiking there.

I therefore decided to head next to Lake Kissimmee State Park. Despite the similar name to the destination of my first trip, the two parks are not close to each other. Where Kissimmee Prairie Preserve is two hours southeast of my home via the Florida Turnpike, Lake Kissimmee State Park is 90 minutes south, near the Lake Wales Ridge and west of the lake for which it is named. Where Kissimmee Prairie Preserve sits entirely in a flat plain of palmetto, Lake Kissimmee is much more forested, and I was starting to adore trees and wanted to spend more time in the forest. I had also already hiked there, having discovered Lake Kissimmee State Park while day hiking to prepare for the trip to Kissimmee Prairie Preserve.

Lake Kissimmee State Park is a hidden gem. Where *LL* feels like a playground, Lake Kissimmee feels more like a natural oasis of forest. A former cattle ranch with a living history exhibit where *cowmen* (don't call them cowboys) entertain kids on weekends, the park borders the lake for which it is named only on its northeast corner. The rest of the park sits among a forest of pine pockmarked with fields of palmetto. It also teems with wildlife. There are plenty of deer, and its proximity to the lake provides for not-so-rare sightings of bald eagles and osprey. You know immediately what you're in for once you pass through the gate, as a winding paved road coasts for several miles through a nest of tall pine and oak.

Lake Kissimmee was also where I was introduced to hikers only trails, although its popularity with the RV set means that you'll see more than a fair share of bicycles and even the occasional golf cart defying the rules. Whereas the trails at Kissimmee Prairie Preserve and *LL* are wide, straight, and easily navigated even in the dark, the trails at Lake Kissimmee are narrow and winding, and therefore provide more of the Hansel and Gretel feel. The park is far removed from any metropolitan area. So aside from the loud grind of outboard motors of bass boats and airboats that occasionally pass by on the lake and the soothing bovine chatter from cattle on nearby ranches, you feel much further away from city folk. There is also an observation tower with views of the lake and forest and a well-appointed camp store near the trailheads.

Lake Kissimmee has two main hikers only loops exceeding six miles each that both have a backcountry campsite. I had previously day hiked the shorter North Loop because the slightly longer Buster Island Loop was reputed to be muddy in spots. For my backpacking trip in February, I chose to do the more highly reputed Buster Island Loop, the risk of mud notwithstanding. Most of the 6.9-mile Buster Island Loop sits in a hammock of pine and live oak surrounding open farmland for the living history exhibit and adjacent palmetto fields, with three lakes in the distance surrounding the island on which the trail sits. On the map, the forested hammock is narrow. But the trail meanders through the hammock in a way that hides the limits of the forest, and you therefore feel like you're much deeper in the woods than you actually are. The campsite sits almost halfway down the trail and therefore allowed me to hike comfortably more distance than in my prior trip, and I elected the longer 3.8-mile leg for the hike in.

As a testament to my wife, she had no problem when the best weather window landed squarely on February 14th. We've never been into hallmark holidays, so I spent Valentine's Day alone in the forest.

As much as I admired Kissimmee Prairie Preserve, I enjoyed Lake Kissimmee much more. My hike in went through the more forested stretch of the Buster Island Loop, through miles of dreamland woods with big live oaks and their sprawling horizontal and diagonal limbs covered in lichen, bromeliads, and moss hugging each turn of the trail. Although the afternoon sun was bright and a bit hot, I was shaded almost the entire way, and I was soothed during the hottest part of the hike in by cool breezes. The pack did feel heavier, but I had no problem cooling down when I reached the campsite.

The campsite was also a gem. Sitting a short distance off the main loop and connected by a short connector trail through dense brush, the campsite was surrounded by tall pine and the sprawling limbs of live oaks. There were also

Campsite at Lake Kissimmee State Park, February 14, 2024.

patches of flat open ground a comfortable distance from the picnic tables and fire pit, so I was easily able to find a secluded space for bedtime star gazing framed by live oak boughs.

I arrived shortly before dusk, so as soon as I finished setting up camp, it was time to walk further down the trail to find a good spot to watch the sunset. I did not find any west facing options, but three quarters of a mile down the trail, I found a south-facing pocket on the forest edge facing a grassy prairie framed by moss hanging from live oaks that reminded me of my campsite at Kissimmee Prairie Preserve. I stayed until a half-hour after the mosquitoes appeared and forced me to pull out my bug repellant wipe. By the time I left to return to camp, it was starting to become dark enough to require vigilance to find the connector trail.

When I reached the connector trail, I could not resist continuing back up the main loop and retracing my steps from the hike in. Before I reached the connector, I could already see the crescent moon and stars shining through the live oaks and the fluffy tops of the longleaf pines. I knew there were more tall pines past the connector trail, and I could not resist the urge to continue further to hunt for perfect pictures of the moon and stars. The owls were back, and I spent at least 30 minutes after full darkness before returning to camp.

It was on the walk back that I had my failure for the trip. I had become a bit too confident night hiking on the wider and more familiar trails at *LL*, and I had not yet realized at that time how badly I needed glasses. Even though I had hiked this way before during the day, I missed the connector trail to my campsite in the dark and walked almost a half-mile past it, perhaps because I was moving too quickly in my

Night sky at Lake Kissimmee State Park, February 14, 2024.

excitement. When I realized my mistake, I turned around, took a mental chill pill, slowed my roll, retraced my steps, and looked much harder for the connector trailhead. I found it before too long, but I took note of a new lesson: Do not hike at night in dense, unfamiliar terrain.

The evening was otherwise spectacular. I had by now gotten the hang of my camp stove and freeze-dried dinners, and the mosquitoes ignored me after dark. The low humidity of the passing front brought cooler temperatures and an ease of fire maintenance. I had now learned to supplement my lighter load of cheater kiln-dried logs with fallen branches from my campsite. After taking my time with a battery-powered candle lit dinner, I had a long, contemplative fire, half of which I spent naked again after my yuppie shower. As a bonus, the sky was clear and the moon was hidden among the pines, so I saw twice as many stars that night as I had at Kissimmee Prairie Preserve. While my campfire continued to burn easily, I moved my camp stool to the clearing near my campsite and gazed for an hour at the jet-black sky whose pinpricks of white shone like tiny polka dots on a flowing black gown. *This* was serenity. Time stood still.

I have no idea when I went to bed, I only know that it was the best I had slept in months, even though I'm sure I fought slumber to stare at the night sky for as long as I could. When I awoke in the morning, I told my bladder to go back to sleep and turned my sleeping chamber into a chaise lounge and positioned myself to savor every second of the sunrise. I took my time getting out of the tent, then faced the rising sun as I made my morning oatmeal and coffee. I returned to the log beside my campfire and propped my feet

Pine tree growing out of a split live oak, on the Buster Island Loop at Lake Kissimmee State Park, February 15, 2024.

atop it while relaxing on my camp stool, dodging beams of sun slowly moving through the pines as I drank the jet fuel coffee and savored tiny bites of oatmeal and melted M&Ms. This was not a morning to rush, and I took my time breaking camp.

The hike out was cooler, lighter, and sunnier as I passed through the more open stretch of trail passing through the palmettos. When I reached the car after 3.1 miles of hiking, I knew it was too soon to go home. I dropped my tent, sleeping bag, and air mattress off at my car, grabbed the fresh bottle of water and lunch I had waiting in a cooler, and moved on to the 4-mile Gobbler Ridge Loop Trail that reached Lake Kissimmee. I finally found sugar sand and the mud I had not seen on the loop, but fortunately saw no gators on the muddiest stretch abutting the lake. I had lunch shirtless on a bench beside the lake and saw my first bald eagle of the season, along with a longleaf pine growing in the split trunk of a live oak. After finally reaching my car around lunch time, I stopped by the camp store and grabbed a soda, then spent one last half-hour atop the observation tower and gazed at the distant lake and the tops of the pines I now adored. This was the best trip so far.

As with the first trip to Kissimmee Prairie Preserve, I had long before decided where I would do my two-night trip, and when my backpacking adventures began to appear to follow a script, I initially anticipated that the two-nighter would be my last trip of the season. A weather window popped up the following Wednesday, and the campsites I needed for my planned route were available when I needed them. Rather than wait until later, I decided that I would next do a two-night trip to Myakka River State Park.

Myakka River State Park is one of Florida's older and bigger state parks and parts were built by the Civilian Conservation Corps established by Franklin Roosevelt to provide temporary public employment to the victims of the Great Depression.[15] Pretty log cabins built by the CCC still stand near the park entrance.[16] At the time it opened, Myakka River State Park was 22 miles west of Sarasota and its sprouting community of homes and businesses.[17] With the growth of the Tampa Bay area in the decades since, Myakka River is now slowly being swallowed by suburban sprawl, but it's still big enough to provide a unique place to hike and backpack.

Most tourists know Myakka River State Park for its alligators. A busy gift shop and lunch location sits near a water control structure surrounded by large and often full parking lots and picnic tables. The RV and parking lot campers spend hours watching the gators, particularly in the summer and fall when the water of the Myakka River is high and the gators are more plentiful. Even on weekdays, the park's paved roads are congested with bicycles and slow-moving cars that can be frustrating for the non-senior citizen drivers who try to make their way around. Its big attraction for me was its 39-mile hikers only Myakka Hiking Trail with multiple backcountry campsites and intersecting cross trails that make Myakka River the perfect destination for trying a multi-day solo backpacking trip for the first time.

The Myakka Hiking Trail is a roughly octagonal loop stretching from west to east from the backcountry trailhead sitting across a paved road from the river and its adjacent cypress flats. It has six backcountry campsites along its loop path, some of which have water pumps to allow multi-night backpackers to avoid having to cache water. Most of the terrain inside the loop is flat palmetto prairie like Kissimmee Prairie Preserve, and a video at the visitor's center depicts a reenactment of Florida's earliest white settlers crossing the prairie on foot or in wagons looking for new land upon which to make their homesteads. The prairie and much of the trail itself flood during the rainy summer and fall months, so the Myakka Trail is only really an option in the winter and spring. As I would find out, parts of the trail are submerged in ankle-deep muddy water even during the dry months. But it is one of the biggest loop trails in Florida sitting within a state park with the security of park rangers available for a quick response to emergencies.

I decided to keep my first two-nighter somewhat easy and limit it to 11.2 miles in 3 days, beginning on Day 1 with a 2.2 mile hike east to the Mossy Hammock campsite on the northwest edge of the loop, continuing on 3.6 miles via a connector trail to the Bee Island campsite on Day 2, then finishing with a 5.4 mile hike back west and north to the trailhead on Day 3. It was to be my most ambitious attempt at solo backpacking to date. I loaded up with as much water as I could carry—4 liters—but because I knew I had a water pump waiting for me on Day 2, I also visited REI one more time to buy a water filter and collapsible one-liter bottle as a backup. I counted the hours as the six days passed between my return from Lake Kissimmee to the climactic trip that I had been dreaming about for two months. I was tickled that I would be making that dream come true weeks before I originally anticipated.

But I had one more panic attack to endure before I hit the trail. This time it was on the drive to Sarasota, and it was a big one.

The drive from my home to Myakka River State Park was almost entirely on interstates, beginning with an hour-long stretch on I-4 from Orlando west to Tampa, and then joining I-75 east of Tampa and driving south a bit more than an hour to Sarasota before leaving the Interstate and heading east for less than 10 miles. Although I had driven on I-4 since rekindling my relationship with depression and anxiety, I had not been in the kind of traffic I faced heading south on I-75 at noon that Wednesday. It wasn't so much bumper-to-bumper, but instead pockets of congestion, where you had to struggle to make your way through retirees and people texting while driving, speed forward to the next blockage, then weave your away around slow-moving drivers too distracted or lazy to pass each other.

It was at this point that I had a difficult run-in with one of those immutable laws of human nature. People who drive big Ford F-150-type trucks do not pass. It's a scientific law. There are occasional freaks of nature who drive such vehicles and do move out of the way when in the passing lane. But they are so rare that I can remember each time I've seen one, like an albino alligator. And they don't care who they piss off in the process.

Of course, most of the people who drive F-150s are extremely friendly. That's one of the main reasons I enjoy visiting states where such drivers congregate like Georgia and Alabama—they're among the nicest people in the world. But a small percentage of them, typically male drivers of F-150s between the ages of 17 and 35, can become overly aggressive when provoked, even after they initially provoke road rage themselves by unnecessarily camping in passing lanes beside slow drivers. Throughout my life, I've had too many such drivers than I care to remember pull up beside me, roll down their windows, shout obscenities, and make aggressive hand gestures with fists and middle fingers. I always ignore them and then jet past them when the opportunity arises. I've also had a few try to cut in front of me and slam their brakes.

On the I-75 leg of the drive to Sarasota, I encountered one such psycho in a red F-150. In fairness, I had passed many people perhaps too close to their bumpers just before he found me. It couldn't be helped. There were few holes for passing between the pockets of congestion, and like a good running back who would prefer to not be hit, I found running lanes and hit them aggressively, even if the drivers I had to pass were on their phones or leaving little space.

To be candid, I do not even remember what I did to this driver. I don't remember passing a red F-150, but I know that I had passed a few drivers aggressively, and he may have been affected by my efforts, even if only indirectly. All I know is that I quickly had a crappy red F-150 driven by a guy with a dirty tank top and missing teeth roll up beside me, roll down his window, shout something that presumably was not a holiday greeting, and veer toward me as if to sideswipe me.

At first, I had no problem with this. I quickly weaved by two other drivers to open space and hit the gas, leaving the entire glob of automotive molasses behind. But within a minute, I saw the F-150 barreling toward me at high speed, and I soon reached another blob of slow-moving molasses, and this time I couldn't get through. Mr. KKK had not yet said his peace.

I weaved my way through several more vehicles and deeper into the blob, trying to avoid him. But by now, Mr. KKK was passing much more aggressively than I was, and the slower drivers were now getting out of his way to let him pass out of fear. This time he was also trying to provoke me like an orca playing with a seal. He would tease me by pulling beside me and leaving a car length and a half behind the driver in front of him to bait me into trying to pass him, then as soon as I tried, he would speed up to close the hole and feign to weave back into me. He would then stay there and not pass, noticeably irritating the drivers behind him who were now stuck behind both of us. This went on for 10 minutes, and I was starting to hear honking from behind. This did not phase Mr. KKK. But it did not bother me either, so I slowed my roll, knowing that it's best once provoking a redneck bear to play dead and not look it in the eye.

This made the bear even more angry. He sped up, cut in front of me, and slammed his brakes, almost causing a multi-car pile-up. At this point, I started to get scared. Normally, I would get angry—very, very fucking angry. But I was not myself at that moment, and the feeling I had was abject terror and fear for my life. I would have pulled over, but I knew that's what the bear wanted, so he could drag me outside the protection of my steel and glass bubble or at least break the window.

Of course, because he drove an F-150, he was a shitty driver and could not accelerate as quickly as I could. I therefore waited until the right moment came. Once a hole opened ahead, I accelerated quickly around Mr. KKK, then threaded through traffic until I found an older driver going 10 miles below the speed limit. I then went right behind him as he approached stop-and-go traffic, and I stuck to his rear bumper like glue, occasionally giving a friendly wave and smile through my tears to let him know I wasn't an enemy. Eventually Mr. KKK caught up, but I skillfully sped up and slowed down to prevent even a half-car length between me and Mr. Slow. Mr. KKK was not going to get in front of me again, no matter what. This lasted another 10 minutes, even after space in front of Mr. Slow opened and our little group still slowed down to 35 miles per hour. At this point, I presume Mr. Slow just wanted us both to pass so he could avoid witnessing my imminent death through his rearview mirror.

I still had more than 40 miles to go before my exit off I-75, and I know from experience that lunatics like Mr. KKK follow other drivers way past their own exits. I almost called 911, but I still didn't have glasses and was too panicked to try to dial my phone while trying to keep Mr. KKK from wrecking me. I also considered exiting I-75 and driving directly to a police station, but I had no idea where to go, and the last thing I wanted was to be stuck at a stop light with

Mr. KKK able to leave his hovel to attack me with firearms and fists.

So I instead stuck to my instincts. I waited until Mr. KKK, now sitting in the middle of three lanes, became stuck behind so much traffic that he couldn't pass to chase. Finally, I saw a quick set of holes develop ahead of the pocket of slow-moving traffic in front of me with miles of open space ahead. Once I got to a point where I doubted Mr. KKK could follow, I hit the gas and passed Mr. Slow, weaved my car through the remaining vehicles like a needle sewing a NASCAR merit badge, and floored it to 100 when I reached blue sky until I caught up with the next pocket of slow-moving traffic. I then slowed down to civility speed, *politely* passed more cars, and positioned myself in front of a barrier of traffic that would have been too thick for Mr. KKK to chase me through. I then kept one eye constantly on my rearview mirror, looking for a red blur and listening for gun shots.

After 15 minutes of not seeing Mr. KKK, I was able to slow my pulse to just above standard heart attack speed; I was still so alarmed that I was still afraid to drive, but I was far more afraid to pull over and risk that he'd find me. I determined to use every ounce of courage I had left to drive straight to Myakka River State Park and then decompress once I got there with as much nicotine as needed.

Mr. KKK never caught up to me, but that did not make the drive any easier. Violent paranoia scorched my blood and polluted my mind. Even music could not soothe me. This is not the way the DMV wants you to drive. Of course, the silver lining was that I drove much more calmly the rest of the way and provoked no other drivers. But I was living a nightmare.

The worst part was that right when I finally got off the interstate and got onto the long two-lane road to the park, a red F-150 pulled up right behind me. It took me several minutes to discern that he wasn't waiving fists or firearms and had glasses, sleeves, and all of his teeth and was therefore clearly not Mr. KKK. But I still sped far ahead of him just in case. I never would have been happier to be pulled over by a cop.

That was not an ideal way to begin my first two-night solo backpacking trip.

Myakka River State Park, February 21, 2024.

Florida National Scenic Trail at the Croom Tract of the Withlacoochee State Forest, February 28, 2024.

CHAPTER EIGHT

A February to Remember

Once I reached Myakka River State Park, I choked down half my nicotine vape, squeezed out a few drops in the restroom, and eventually calmed down enough to look a bit normal when I checked into my campsites. A visitor's center was across the parking lot from the ranger station at the entrance, and I had several hours before I had to set off, so I went inside to get some ecological and historical context. The visitors' center had a small theater with five short videos on local history and fauna, and I watched every video as I slowly became able to enjoy the day again. I then headed to the crowded point with the river lookout and gift shop where I found no alligators. I ate the sandwich I had prepared at home, and when I felt the time was right, I headed to the trailhead.

I became instantly elated and focused as soon as I found the trailhead and readied myself for two days in the suburban backcountry. But I was not yet sufficiently calm to find the correct turn to connect north on the Myakka Trail loop. In fairness, it was probably because I had not yet learned a basic fact that all backpackers know—that two blazes stacked atop each other means that you're approaching a junction. I would not learn what this means for several more weeks, and it's a wonder I didn't get lost more often. While walking on a jeep road toward where the Myakka Trail crosses, I noted the stacked blazes signaling me to prepare to turn and wondered why there were two pretty blazes rather than just one and continued strolling. When I eventually realized (again) that I had missed a turn about a half mile too late, I retraced my steps. My hike in thus ended up being 3.1 miles rather than 2.2.

But the hike in was great nonetheless, and it helped me to finally forget about the panicky drive to Sarasota. Just like the Buster Island Loop at Lake Kissimmee State Park, much of the Myakka Trail sits in a hammock surrounding the huge prairie, so the hike between the trailhead and the Mossy Hammock campsite was forested and therefore shady and cool. A few parts were muddy, but on Day 1 the mud was not difficult to skirt around, so I never stepped in mud that rose above my shoelaces. By the time I arrived at camp, I was still awake enough to get to work quickly on my campsite.

The Mossy Hammock campsite sits, as its name suggests, at the edge of a hammock of palms and live oaks near the adjacent prairie to the east, but not close enough to see through for sunrises over the prairie. Although it has three campsites, they are nestled close to each other, and I had all three campsites to myself. The most notable features of the campsites on the Myakka Trail are the tall, thick poles with hooks on them. There are also no picnic tables, but instead wooden stumps with flat tops and bottoms for use as tables for cooking stoves near each fire pit. The presumptive reason for these is that the campsites flood during the summer and fall and can be muddy even during the dry season. The legs of a wooden picnic table would rot, and the poles with hooks provide dry places to hang your backpack at night if your tent, like mine, is too small to fit extra gear.

Mossy Hammock's three campsites were comprised of two sites adjacent to the prairie and one set comfortably back and slightly uphill. The prettiest site and the best for viewing stars was too close to the prairie and was partially flooded, so I moved on. The other prairie-side campsite was the biggest, but it had been trashed by the rednecks who had last stayed there. They had presumably wheeled in too much gear, including a huge camouflage tarp big enough to see from space (if it weren't camouflaged), and their bulldozer apparently had a flat tire because they chose to abandon their tarp at the campsite, along with the box it came in and its other paper contents, bits of rope, cigarette butts, and boxes. I was not impressed. I picked the cleaner, more inland campsite.

As annoyed as I was at the prior rednecks' rudeness, I did not think the next campers should have to deal with their mess. I cut down the heavy tarp, dragged it to the flooded front campsite, folded it, and placed the other trash in a pile near the flooded campsite's firepit. I then called the park office and told the rangers about the mess and that it was too heavy for me to carry out, and they told me a park ranger would eventually come by to get it. I was not trying to tattle, but I also did not want these rangers thinking that I backpacked this way. They understood.

The rednecks did me a favor because I enjoyed the default last option better than I likely would have the other tent sites. This was the only time during my backpacking odyssey that I was forced to sleep less than 15 feet from my fire pit, but I didn't mind a bit. I was surrounded by palm trees and live oaks, literally hugged by the forest, and the moonlit night was barely visible through the canopy. After the sun fell, I felt like I was camping inside a cave.

However, before the night arrived, I had to do my obligatory search for a sunset spot, so I walked to the nearby prairie and had my first glimpse of the long, flat expanse of palmetto with a dusting of the tops of palm and pine trees in the distance. Having not gone far after the lesson about night hiking I learned at Lake Kissimmee, I instead watched the sun set over my campsite, but then scurried back to camp before I had to worry about getting lost in the dark.

Dinner on Night 1 would be most notable for the company. Because I did not have a picnic table, I chose to use my second firewood tarp as a picnic blanket, and I even used old shoestrings to tie a third of one side over the middle third, to have a moisture cover if the humidity threatened to dampen my gear or my firewood. For comfort, I also pulled out my clothes bag to use as a cushion to lay upon my firewood. It was soon thereafter that I started hearing rattling in the bushes that sounded too big to be lizards. The first opossum appeared soon thereafter.

As I mentioned before, opossums are not afraid of novice backpackers, especially when they are well fed by trash left by sloppy parking-lot campers like the rednecks who stayed at Mossy Hammock before I arrived. Several opossums approached me without fear and were only slightly annoyed at the beating of my fire stick on my kitchen stump. They had learned that the really good food was near the white guys. I ate dinner that night before dark, so they did not approach me at that time. But after I started my fire and had my back to my picnic tarp which was covering my clothes and firewood less than three feet behind me, I turned to find a bold opossum rummaging under the folded tarp flap and trying to drag my bag of kindling into the bushes. I did not let a burning fire stick touch the opossum's ass, but I made sure to make him think a hot probe was coming if he came back. He got the hint and stayed away until after the fire went out.

But I still had a nice peaceful night tending the fire, and because of how my drive to the park went, I cut out early and went inside the tent around 11:00. For the first hour when I tried to fall asleep, I listened to the palmettos rattle with what sounded like rodent sarcasm. I had to put in my ear plugs to sleep. But sleep well I did.

The next morning brought bright sunshine at dawn, and I awoke early enough to see the first tremors of the sunrise. By the time I finished a douchey DJ video for my wife of the paradise surrounding my tent, I noticed for the first time that a palm tree was growing from the split trunk of the live oak closest to my fire pit. I was where I belonged. I got up and enjoyed an easy breakfast before preparing for the 3.6-mile hike to Bee Island that I expected to be easy. Although it was dry, it was not that easy.

During that hike, I was in the sunny palmetto prairie with no shade. Of course, it was mid-February and was therefore cool, and I had prepared with sunscreen. I also gaped at the horizon ahead of me, where the tiny horizontal line of palm trees at the far end of the prairie ahead shimmered like a mirage. Every now and then, a pine tree broke up the monotony of the sea of knee-high palm fronds. But the pine trees were sporadic, and so was the shade. By the time I reached the connector trail that left the Myakka Loop for the shortcut to Bee Island with only one mile left until the next campsite, I was feeling legitimately hot and thirsty. As I cut through dense foliage to reach the campsite, I was ready for shade and a break.

The Bee Island campsite is an elevated piece of land in the middle of the prairie that is slower to flood than the prairie itself. I thankfully did not see any bees. It is much bigger than Mossy Hammock and similarly has three campsites, of which two are nestled against the prairie with another being set in privacy further inland. I also quickly found the water pump, and although I initially struggled to raise its contents from the aquifer, I eventually discerned that the jugs of yellow water were meant to prime the pump, and I soon raised cold water from the icy depths that felt incredible on my scalp in the early afternoon heat.

I initially struggled with the decision of which site to take. Each campsite was bigger than the spots at Mossy Hammock. The two prairie-side sites had excellent views of the prairie, but they had little shade and little cover, which meant little privacy if others arrived. One of the prairie-side spots looked directly into the inland site and vice versa, which meant no privacy at all if another camper took that prairie-side spot. I was too tired before lunch to set up my tent, so I had lunch in the shade to think about where specifically to sleep.

Just as I found the energy to lay down the tarp for my tent, a parking lot camper arrived towing a wagon full of stuff. He had trudged a few miles down a sugar sand jeep road and looked tired. I doubt he was excited to see me, as I had no shirt and looked like a homeless person. In the most polished, college-educated vernacular I could muster, I told him about the three campsites and that I was looking for privacy and was thus setting up camp at the inland site and offered to show him the other sites. He took the more secluded prairie-side spot sight unseen. He clearly wanted privacy as well, and it was probably the prettiest spot of the three anyway. Aside from passing him on my way out to sunset hike later that evening, I never saw him again.

By the time I was done setting up my tent, I was exhausted, and even if I had the energy to day hike during peak afternoon heat, I didn't want to waste the water. I took my opossum-unfriendly tarp and laid it in the shade of a live oak, then rested and drank the last of my *ass juice* (tap water polluted with mixed berry electrolyte tablets that tastes like the nickname suggests). While resting during peak afternoon heat, I gazed at the tops of two particularly majestic longleaf pine trees at the edge of the island.

As usual, I eventually became restless, but I was nearing my last one and a half liters of water, and I still had more than five miles of hiking with gear the next morning and another dinner and breakfast that required 24 additional ounces of water. It was time to test the water filter. I returned to the pump, tried to not disturb my neighbor, and jacked a liter of yellow water that smelled like rotten eggs into the collapsible bottle onto which I screwed my water filter. The mechanics were simple: You just squeeze the bottle and press water through the filter, which comes out in a slight trickle, but which eventually fills an empty Nalgene bottle. My original plan was to use this water only to cook. But when I got back to camp, I decided to use my digestive system as a guinea pig and tried a swallow and hoped I would not soon have diarrhea.

The pump water tasted as bad as it smelled. To call it metallic would be far too complimentary. But it was ice cold, I was overheated, and it did not make me throw up. I returned to the pump and pumped out enough to fill one more Nalgene bottle and continued drinking liberally without negative consequences.

This also meant I could finally do some day hiking, but my options were limited. I could either take one of several sandy jeep roads nearby and destroy my legs before the 5.4-mile hike out, or I could head further down the trail to scout out my hike for the next day. I chose the latter and went one and a half miles down the opposite connector trail and the Myakka Trail before turning around, to avoid any risk of fatiguing out.

I arrived in time for my best dinner so far, chicken coconut curry, something I would never touch in the real world because of its vegetables. A big reason people like to come to Myakka is that on the beach of Bee Island on the edge of the prairie, the sunset views are 360 degrees for miles in every direction, and being close to the Gulf of Mexico, the sky that evening was painted after sunset in colors you only see near an ocean. A line of wide, wispy clouds laid across the sky like a breaking wave, painted yellow on the west, fading blue on the east, and orange on the breakers themselves. As the day faded into night, the moon rose early like a dull second sun between a pair of longleaf pine halfway across the prairie. Although we were close to the cities on the bay, the stars were still bright.

It was so glorious an evening that I didn't mind that the humidity dampened my last kiln-dried log. For the first time on my odyssey, I could not start a fire. On the bright side, this spared me from an awkward moment if my neighbor decided to stop by to chat while I tended a campfire wearing nothing but a smile after my yuppie shower. Besides, no bugs were out, and I was happy to go to bed early with the smell of curry and rotten eggs on my breath. I had now gone more than 36 hours without brushing my teeth or applying deodorant. It was time to take those smells into my tent. Sleep came slowly after hours of star gazing from bed. I was beginning to really adore sleeping under the stars.

I woke up early enough to see another postcard sunrise from within the tent and shot another euphoric douchey DJ video for my wife. Once-in-a-lifetime sunrises were now becoming as routine on the backpacking trails of Florida as they were beautiful. With a mostly shaded hike out ahead of me and a desire to hit the congested traffic on I-75 north late enough after lunch to avoid the stress I'd had *en route*, I took my time with breakfast and savored the aging morning. It was not easy to say goodbye to Bee Island.

Once I reached the forested main trail, I finally encountered the first water during my backpacking odyssey that slowed me down. Being closer to the river, this section of the trail already had football field stretches of ankle-deep water that could not be avoided. Had I done the trail in reverse direction and had these longer, wetter miles on Day 1, it might have made the adventure less enjoyable. But I knew I had less than 2 hours of hiking before reaching my car and ending my expedition, so I embraced the challenge and kept moving. It was fun to finally have an obstacle to overcome.

Then about halfway through the final Day 3 hike out, I came to the payoff for the trip when I noticed the distinct "FT" logo made to look like a camp shelter. The next stretch was managed by the Florida Trail Association. Although I had bought Sandra Friend and John Keatley's *The Florida Trail Guide*[18] from REI, I had not yet looked at it closely because it contained precious little information about state parks. But I would no longer ignore that book after finishing with this stretch of trail. The Florida Trail Association (FTA) is a statewide collection of volunteers that maintains the Florida National Scenic Trail (Florida Trail for short), a 1,400-mile stretch of continuous trails stretching from the Everglades north and west to the western tip of Florida's panhandle. FTA volunteers meticulously maintain the Florida Trail and adjacent loop trails or trails of interest throughout Florida by building bridges, clearing paths, and restoring the Florida Trail's famous orange blazes. You always know when you're on the Florida Trail, not just by its blazes, but because its hikers only trails are more thoughtfully designed, better maintained, and more beautiful than other trails.

The portion of the trail I reached with just under three miles to go to return to my car was not part of the Florida

Trail—the closest portions of the Florida Trail lie far east and north of Sarasota—but it was maintained by the FTA, and it was particularly gorgeous and dry. It weaved through the prettiest palm and live oak hammock I saw, and the trail was so well-maintained that you barely needed to look for blazes. I had initially looked at FTA materials at my local REI store only out of general interest while thinking they were for thru hikers that I was far from becoming. After completing this stretch, "Florida Trail" became a buzz term that I looked for in my guides, as "hikers only" had become since my trip to Lake Kissimmee State Park. This lovely stretch of trail was a marvelous way to end my only multi-night trip of my first backpacking season.

When I finally reached the trailhead and my car, I felt a considerable sense of accomplishment, although I couldn't help but notice how much energy I still had left and wondered if I'd cheated myself by not hiking more miles. I also smelled worse than I had in years, but I had left a travel-sized bottle of shampoo in the car for this moment, and I had plenty of the smelly pump water to spare. I stripped down to my underwear right along the side of the paved road, and as retirees passed and awkwardly diverted their gazes, I scrubbed shampoo into my scalp, let it run down my chest and back, and rinsed with smelly water. It felt glorious to be a fraction less dirty.

Of course, I still had a long stressful drive ahead of me, and the last drive on interstates had been memorable for the wrong reasons. My air-conditioning also seemed to no longer work. With considerable trepidation, I made my way back onto I-75 north with my windows rolled down and drove the speed limit without passing. But I still hit massive traffic as I approached Tampa, worse than I had driven through on the way down. I was so hot and paranoid that I missed the turn onto I-4 east. I apparently have a problem with connections.

When I looked for a new route home on my phone to avoid turning around, I noticed that I could instead take State Road 50 all the way back to my home in Winter Garden. I knew that the road passed through forest and was more rural, which perfectly suited my new relaxed pace, and the drive was hot but soothing. As far as I could tell, I had never been on this stretch of highway before. But it would not be long before I would drive there again.

When I returned from Myakka River State Park, I was still not ready to return to work. Panic attacks like the one I had at the gastroenterologist's office had become more frequent. I'd had a similar attack in the waiting room of my general care doctor shortly thereafter, and then another about a week later in the waiting room of another medical office. After my breakthrough at the gastroenterologist's office, I dealt with these panic attacks in a healthier way. Rather than wait for the attacks to come on, I told the receptionists when I arrived that I was being treated for anxiety and warned them about the possibility that I might get antsy if forced to wait for too long. Despite my proactive approach, I still experienced the early signs of a panic attack, including the racing panicky thoughts and muscle contractions. But once again, both receptionists expressed sympathy—one even referred to a family member who suffered from bipolar depression—and both went out of their way to get me in as quickly as they could. So those attacks didn't ruin my day.

But the bad panic attack on the drive to Sarasota was not particularly exceptional. I was still brooding about work, the conflict with my out-of-state friend, and conflicts with family, and I was still waking up every morning at 5 a.m. despite only sleeping three or four hours. One morning shortly after the trip to Myakka River State Park, following a minor disagreement with my wife, I got so angry that I extended my morning walk around my neighborhood to an hour and a half without warning my wife or taking my phone to let her know where I was, which caused her considerable concern. I was still not yet noticing any effect from the Prozac. Although I was seeing some payoff from my efforts to work on my mental health, it was hard to appreciate my progress with so little sleep and so much negativity still swirling around my brain.

Despite all of that, I decided to take another risk. As the thrill of my backpacking adventures continued to build, I was aching to tell people. Perhaps it was because of the positive attention I had received the prior summer and autumn for my weight loss, but I felt a profound sense of accomplishment and discovery that I wanted to share with friends. I was also beginning to get a bit lonely. But I also feared that no one would understand or care for the same reasons that led me to not post about backpacking on my Facebook page. I also knew that it would be hard to share details about the number of backpacking trips I had taken in such a brief period of time without making the listener wonder if I was still working. I was not yet ready to tell friends about my sabbatical, much less my mental health problems.

But I decided to make an exception. I had not been surprised that my Gator football friend and I had not reconnected since the end of the college football season. We'd had that falling out the prior spring and a rough time at the Florida-Georgia game, but that didn't seem to bother him. As typical guys, we often go months at a time without reaching out to each other, so it was no surprise that I had not heard from him. But then unexpectedly, shortly before I left for the trip to Kissimmee Prairie Preserve, he sent me a text asking how I was doing.

His text touched me, as it arrived while I was feeling lonely and forgotten. I also knew he was equipped to at least understand, if not appreciate, my backpacking odyssey. He was far more of an outdoorsman than me. He hunts alligators in the fall, lives on a spring fed lake and uses his boat regularly and spends summer weekends deep sea fishing off the Atlantic Coast. We had also hiked together before. So I decided to take a chance and tell him about what I was doing.

Rather than limit how much I told him about backpacking, I told him about the sabbatical, too. I was far more reluctant to share this. Perhaps because of my illness at the time, I had a paralyzing fear that my friends would dismiss the entire notion of mental illness and the profession of psychiatry, particularly if they abided to certain religious and political convictions that this friend shared. But I also vaguely recalled him referring sympathetically to other friends who suffered from depression or anxiety, so I was willing to take a chance.

The Saturday after I got back from Myakka River State Park, I sent the friend several text messages, where I began by telling him about my backpacking, but then added that I'm on a health-related sabbatical with my boss's approval, and I asked him to not tell anyone because he was the first person other than my sister that I had yet told. I was perhaps a bit too vague for my own good. To avoid being too graphic in case I got a negative response, I described my emotional ailment as "anxiety and panic attacks" rather than something more clinical, and I mentioned nothing about my history of suicidal depression. For this reason, texts he sent later made clear that he believed that my sabbatical was more for pleasure. But he did respond positively. He told me he cared about me and hoped I would get well soon, and he agreed to keep my secret between us.

I didn't really appreciate it at the time, but opening up about my mental illness to a friend and to receptionists was an important step to getting better.

I also wanted to get back to the trail as soon as possible. Having by now begun to see my first backpacking season as life-changing, I had originally assumed the two-nighter at Myakka River State Park would be the climax of my hiking season and possibly my last trip. But I was already searching for weather windows when I returned, and I had not yet challenged myself enough. I also knew it was time to stop confining my gaze to state parks, as there just weren't enough other state parks close enough that had long enough hikers only loops with backcountry campsites. It was now time to consider state forests. State forests were less expensive than the already cheap state parks, as reservations at many backcountry campsites in state forests are only $1.00 per night or even free.

I was also electrified by the FTA trail at Myakka River State Park. I immediately read the introductory chapters of *The Florida Trail Guide* and learned about the Florida National Scenic Trail. After beginning near the Everglades, the Florida Trail circles around Lake Okeechobee as it heads north, and then eventually splits south of Orlando, with one leg continuing east of Orlando near the St. John's River and another leg heading west to the south of Orlando, before turning north and eventually east again north of Tampa. The alternative legs then merge east of Ocala in the Ocala National Forest, before heading north to the east of Gainesville and eventually turning west shortly after passing over I-10 before crossing the Florida panhandle.

Many pristine miles of the western leg of the Florida Trail pass through the Withlacoochee State Forest north of Tampa, through the stretch of forest I drove through on State Road 50 when returning from Myakka River State Park. This stretch of the Florida Trail also links to loop trails of greater distance than the loops found at most state parks. They pass through huge, majestic swaths of hilly pine forest, through the headwaters of slow-moving rivers that drain into the Gulf of Mexico that resemble sets from a Tarzan movie. Several loop trails through the Withlacoochee State Forest also received rave reviews in my guidebooks, and they had just the right amount of greater distance I now wanted.

A weather window arrived during the middle of the final week of February, and I decided to do one more one-nighter on the A and B Loops of the Croom Tract of the Withlacoochee Forest near Brooksville. Sitting on 20,000 acres of state forest land comprising only part of the Florida's largest state forest, the Croom Tract hosts a stretch of the Withlacoochee River on its east side, and live oak and pine-covered hills rise as you move west and north from the river. It is also covered by not only hikers only trails, but also horse trails and mountain bikers only trails. These trails often cross each other, but because of their thoughtful design, horse and mountain bikers need not worry about running over hikers, and hikers don't need to worry about horse hooves and mountain bike tires tearing up their fragile hiking surfaces.

The 11.7-mile route I chose started from a trailhead and parking area on a hill rising above the river approximately five miles west, then headed south and east before turning north just west of the river, reaching PCZ (primitive camp zone) East after 5.1 miles of hiking. This portion also sloped downhill, whereas the longer 6.6-mile return stretch the next day would climb higher hills and would present the toughest challenge I had yet faced. Best of all, more than six miles of the loop would be comprised of the Florida Trail. This would be a wonderful way to end the backpacking season.

The last Wednesday of February, I set out for the Withlacoochee State Forest by backtracking on the relatively traffic-free stretch of rural State Road 50 upon which I had driven only five days earlier. But as I got to within 20 miles of my destination, the path ahead looked ominous, and it only got worse as I approached. Straight ahead lay large

Mossy Hammock campsite, Myakka River State Park, February 21, 2024.

Foggy morning on the Florida National Scenic Trail, at the Croom Tract of the Withlacoochee State Forest, February 29, 2024.

columns of smoke, and the smell of burning wood became more intense the closer I drove to the trailhead.

Controlled forest fires in February are nothing new for Central Floridians, nor, for that matter, are naturally occurring forest fires in other months. Florida not only receives more rainfall than most American states, but also more lightning. The ecosystem has adapted to lightning and even *needs* fire to survive. The cones of many species of pine only open and eject their seeds when burning, and the tall pine trees have bark and sap adapted to protect their lower branchless trunks from fires that burn off brush and other plants, which begin growing again hours after fires burn out. With the encroachment of civilization, natural fires are no longer permitted to burn uncontrollably, but fires must still occur for the forests to flourish. So throughout dry winter months, park rangers and forest managers study weather forecasts, looking for the best winds and humidity to burn parcels of forest, often without public notice.

Forestry officials may have publicized advance notice of their intent to burn a square of forest that included part of the B Loop that day, but I didn't see it, and I'm not sure I would have cared even if I had. When I drove through smoke close to the trailhead and suspected that I may encounter fire in the first miles of my hike in, I naturally became nervous. But I was not going to turn around and go home after having driven almost two hours to get there.

I had several options. A straight, paved road stretched almost directly away from the smoke to a crossing of the Florida Trail just south of my campsite and would have cut several miles off my hike in. I rejected that option immediately because I didn't drive this far to hike on roads. I could also reverse direction and do the longer 6.6-mile stretch on Day 1, then hope any fire was done burning when I hiked through the burning stretch the next morning. But besides being almost double the distance of any hike I'd yet done with 40 pounds on my back, that stretch of trail was hillier than my planned hike. On an afternoon that was already hot and dry, I did not want to push my limits that far. So I took my chances and stuck to the original plan and hoped the fire I smelled and saw was part of the forest that didn't include my trail.

I was sadly disappointed, as about three-quarters of a mile down the trail, right after the trail crossed a wide sandy jeep road, the trail was blocked by fluorescent tape with a small piece of cardboard saying, "Prescribed Burn in Progress 2/28/24." Now I had to make a decision.

Ignoring the sign was obviously not an option. Only a fool would walk into a section of forest known to be on fire. The other options referenced above were now even less palatable. Fortunately, I had a map, and the forest was transected by a checkerboard of north-south and east-west sand roads used by the firefighters that were managing the controlled burn, and I was standing on one of those roads. I did not know exactly where I was, but I knew generally that the burning section was in the southwest corner of my hike, so I was able to narrow my location to two or three possible spots. I also doubted the fire would occupy more than a single square tract cut by the forest roads. I therefore deduced that I could complete my hike by walking east along the sandy road I was now on beside the burning section of forest, then turn right at the next intersection and walk down that road, and I should soon reach the point where the loop trail leaves the burning section and crosses over into forest that was not burning.

After taking a few disgruntled snapshots for *My Secret World*, I started trudging through sugar sand to the intersection I could already see, then started walking up the bisecting road. After several hundred yards, I saw a forest manager wearing a fire-fighting suit approaching on an ATV. He was as friendly as could be, and when I told him what I was doing, he said the trail crossing was just ahead and I would be fine once I reached it. I found the trail about ten minutes later, and this potential day-ending disaster turned into a good story, with a few photos of blackened, smoldering palmetto and tree trunks.

The rest of the hike in was warm and not very shady, but still not difficult because of the downhill slope toward the river. It was also desolate, as I saw only a single trail runner in two hours of hiking.

The payoff came almost four and a half miles into my hike, when I turned north from the westernmost point of my hike and joined the Florida Trail. I could tell instantly that I had reached it because my surroundings changed from just run-of-the-mill gorgeous to mind-blowingly beautiful. As the trail descended and rose through more dense forest and palmetto, the trees became larger and inched closer. At one point, the trail was crossed by a huge live oak several feet in diameter rising more than six feet above the trail like a bridge; even the blaze was painted directly above the trail, as if inviting you to high five it as you passed beneath. I was back on a movie set, and I wished that I had been backpacking on the Florida Trail from the beginning.

When I reached PCZ East a few hours before sunset, I was not particularly blown away. The camping zone was an open stretch of flat ground with only skinny pines and few bushes offering little privacy, even far back from the trail. It was more of a group campsite and was available for reservation by many hikers, although I was the only one there that night. It was also close enough to a paved road to hear engines and see approaching headlights when cars passed at night, although that happened rarely. There was even a strange little headstone with a nearby wind chime, and I wondered if I was camping in a pet cemetery. But I wasn't complaining. I had a few hours of daylight left, so I set up my tent and headed back down the Florida Trail.

After retracing my steps to the point where the B Loop joined the Florida Trail, I found a nearby High-Water Trail and Low-Water Trail joining just ahead. I started down one of them, but I soon started running out of energy and daylight, so I paused briefly at a junction less than two miles from my campsite, then trudged back to camp before dark. When I made it there, I had completed more than eight miles of hiking, five with a 40-pound load in afternoon heat, and my tank was empty. Dinner and fire could wait; I needed to relax for a bit. I placed my backpack on top of the wobbly picnic table, leaned it against my camp stool, and hoped the table wouldn't collapse under my weight as I watched the sunset from my chaise lounge. It did not, and the sunset was charming as usual as Spielberg shot another douchey DJ panoramic video while the evening crickets chirped. Any disappointment I had upon arriving at PCZ East was now gone. I was lying among the pines, and I was very happy to be there.

Dinner was unremarkable. I had run out of my favorite freeze-dried dinners, and with time running out and the REI store being a long drive away, I had settled for chili mac from a less appetizing brand of freeze-dried trail dinners. I was also so tired that I passed on fire, despite having carried a pair of kiln-dried logs that I left wrapped in a paper bag for the next campers. All I wanted was a bed under the stars. I found them and enjoyed the evening just fine.

Because I was sleeping only four hours each night at home, it did not surprise me that I woke up at 4 a.m. and could not fall back to sleep, but I allowed myself a not-so-cold starlit whizz on a pine tree and returned to my sleeping bag as I waited for the day to begin. I wanted to get started early anyway. I had 6.6 miles ahead of me, more than a mile longer than the farthest I'd hiked yet with gear, and this time I was looking forward to hills high enough that they are used by Floridians training for hiking in the Appalachians. I also expected sun and heat, so I wanted to get on the trail before it became too hot. I shot more douchey DJ videos for my wife while having my morning coffee and oatmeal, and I broke camp and resumed my trek on the Florida Trail by 8:45.

This was the most satisfying hike I'd had yet while backpacking. My concerns about sun and heat were misplaced, as the hills were blanketed with a hazy fog that muted the sun's rays and made the forest seem like even more of a dream world. This surprise and a night of rest fueled me through the early flatter sections, and I built momentum as my quads and thighs bristled with veins and growing strength. The backpack felt much lighter than it had earlier in February.

The morning got even better when I reached the hills. Though surely unremarkable to hikers from mountainous states, these karst hills provided elevation that motivated me and views that made the climbs worthwhile. I began looking forward to reaching the crests, as a stationary cyclist in a spinning class looks forward to peak sprints. I began noticing myself smiling as I began fatiguing while reaching the tops of hills. I was now enjoying my exertion as much as the beauty of the Florida Trail.

Perhaps my most pleasant surprises were the trail angels I met while hiking. The first was an older gentleman I saw hanging fluorescent ribbons from trees ahead of me on the trail. He asked about the route I had taken and complimented me when I told him about my sabbatical and backpacking odyssey. He also explained that he was marking the trail for a marathon and invited me to return and participate, beaming with pride about his home forest.

Even better were the trail angels I met next, including the ones with four legs.

Less than one mile before I reached the trailhead, I noticed a straight sand road to my left and realized I was walking parallel to a horse trail. A few minutes later, I saw two large figures beyond the bushes and immediately realized two riders were approaching. Within seconds, I heard rustling and snorting and a somewhat distressed female voice asking who was there. Having learned from my experience during my first encounter with horses at *LL*, I stopped dead in my tracks and immediately called out calmly that I would be happy to stand still until they passed and try to not distress their horses. But after edging closer to me, the voice asked if I could instead come meet them.

When I popped out onto the horse trail, one of the riders explained that my silver backpack cover spooked one of the horses, which was just learning to carry riders. She suspected that the horse thought my pack cover was a wild animal attacking me and was scared for my safety, and it was a new experience that the young horse had not yet endured. She suggested that I stand still while the riders approached slowly, so both horses could inspect my pack cover and confirm that there was nothing to fear. I did exactly that, and these two beautiful mammals came up and sniffed my backpack and my extended palms and nudged me to pet their manes and muscular necks. I'm sure I enjoyed the new experience more than the horses did, and the friendly ladies and their steeds made my week. At a time when I had lost faith in the world around me, these experiences helped put things into perspective. I completed the last mile of the hike—the hardest and hilliest—with a big horsey grin.

By then, the sun had risen to its full glory. If my backpacking season was now over, I had ended it with a challenge and a new sense of pride. My drive home on State Road 50 was much more pleasant than it had been six days earlier.

Live oaks at Lake Kissimmee State Park, February 14, 2024.

CHAPTER NINE

Breakthroughs and Nightmares

I was not sure whether I would backpack again that season after returning from the Withlacoochee State Forest, and I was almost certain I wouldn't do so before my family left for a spring break trip to Arizona on March 15th. We planned to do a lot of hiking in Sedona, and although I wanted to stay in shape for the trip, I did not want to risk injury before hiking on Sedona's stony hills and cliffs. As it turned out, events transpired shortly after I returned from the Withlacoochee Forest that made another backpacking trip during the ensuing two weeks impossible. In fact, I almost had to skip the trip to Arizona.

What ensued between my return from the Withlacoochee State Forest and my departure for Arizona were the most difficult days I've experienced since attempting suicide in 1999 and then enduring the torture of that first week in rehab after leaving inpatient psychiatric care. But I also had my most significant breakthroughs since the return of my depression and anxiety in 2023. The profound discoveries I made about myself—and the adjustment of my medication—

allowed me to learn how to cope with my newly evolved disease and return to work. They also allowed me to retain the sacred place in my life now held by solo backpacking.

It all started with a book and a bad memory. The bad memory came first.

As I mentioned before, I had reconnected with my sister after eight years of not speaking shortly before my depression and anxiety revealed itself again in 2023, and her support helped me cope with my new issues. But our relationship had always been complicated. We hated each other when we were kids, then became close friends when I went to college and she eventually joined me and married one of my best friends from college, but we then grew apart and ultimately suspended our relationship in 2015 and did not reconnect until shortly before my depression and anxiety reemerged. She also endured the trauma of being my main support when I was suicidal in 1999, which was a taxing and unfair burden to place on a senior in college.

Although an explosive fight with my sister during Christmas of 2015 ultimately caused our eight-year break from each other, we had been growing apart for years, largely because of something she did that hurt my feelings that I never told her about. As I've mentioned before, I really, *really* connect with movies and often associate the major events of my life with them. When my sister's wedding arrived in 2002, rather than pick a gift off her registry, I decided to get creative. I spent almost $300 on DVDs of films that had emotional significance to me, including movies that helped me cope with depression during my suicidal years. I then printed and attached labels to each film explaining why it was important to me. I considered this a more personal gift that would allow my sister and her husband and I to bond in a more meaningful way, and I hoped we'd one day watch some of those films together, or perhaps films that had similar significance to them.

Unfortunately, I never heard anything from them about the wedding gift. I obsessed for years about why that occured. Did they lose the gift? Did they not like it? Did they laugh at my childish naivety in sending such an inappropriate wedding gift?

This tortured me for decades. Perhaps not surprisingly, I ultimately chose to believe a painful and negative explanation that painted both myself and them in a negative light and suggested that the close bond I thought we had never existed at all. The closest answer I ever got was when I spent the night on their couch once and, being unable as usual to sleep, searched their entertainment center for movies to watch at 3:00 in the morning and found the films at the back of the bottom drawer, unopened and dusty. This sealed my decision to never mention the gift to them.

But the day before I drove to the Withlacoochee State Forest, I finally shared this bad memory with my sister, in a way that must have shocked her.

Because of our revived connection, I had told my sister about my backpacking adventures as soon as they began, and I also invited her to join my backpacking Facebook group shortly after I created it—she was the only person I invited for almost two months. My sister warned me that she hates Facebook, but I thought I had expressed the importance of my invitation and assumed she would make an exception and accept the invitation to the group. But as the weeks wore on, she still did not accept the invitation, and it drove me nuts. When I could no longer conceal my anger, I sent her a long "WTF" email defending what I perceived to be my own overreaction to her lack of enthusiasm about the Facebook group by telling her about the pain I'd felt all these years about the wedding gift. I then drew parallels between her ignoring the Facebook invitation and ignoring the wedding gift.

Predictably, this did not receive an immediate response, and I suspect my sister began questioning whether it was still a promising idea to resume our relationship. As for me, the pain caused by my sister's seemingly trivial failure to accept a Facebook invitation became the new obsession that distracted me from anything positive in my life. For the moment, I put work and the conflicts with my parents and out-of-state friend on the back burner.

But then a major breakthrough came from a book.

Shortly before I left for the Withlacoochee State Forest, I purchased *The Highly Sensitive Person* by Elaine Aron, PhD[19] and began reading it the day after I returned from the Withlacoochee State Forest. By the time I had finished the introductory chapter, the book had changed my life, and I finished its more than 250 pages in two days. In those sacred pages, Dr. Aron gave me answers to questions that had been disrupting my life for decades.

Dr. Aron, a researcher and clinical psychotherapist, has spent her professional life studying people she describes as *highly sensitive persons* (HSPs). She seems to have chosen that name to avoid offending HSPs, which she believes comprise less than 1/5 of the population.[20] Dr. Aron characterizes HSPs as having four characteristics:

1) HSPs process information more deeply and observe and reflect more before they act, whether consciously or not. This is often construed as taking more time than others to make decisions, but whether made instantly or slowly, HSPs think more before they act.[21]

2) HSPs are more easily overstimulated, in part because of their deeper observation and reflection. This also causes many HSPs, particularly those with depression or anxiety, to wear out and shut down more quickly when overstimulated.[22]

3) HSPs react with greater emotional intensity to their experiences, whether positive or negative, including art and music. As a result, they often have greater empathy. Rather than simply understanding another person's point of view intellectually, they feel more how others feel.[23]

4) HSPs are more sensitive to subtleties in their environment. They're more likely to notice seemingly irrelevant visual cues like body language and facial expressions or tone in communications and react to them.[24]

Dr. Aron notes that high sensitivity should not be confused with *neuroticism*, including certain types of intense anxiety, depression, overattachment, or avoidance of intimacy, which are more often caused by troubled childhoods.[25] Indeed, many HSPs are not neurotic, and many HSPs have healthy childhoods.[26] But HSPs with troubled childhoods also have problems with intense anxiety, depression, overattachment, or avoidance of intimacy, and high sensitivity can make HSPs more vulnerable to such problems—or can make HSPs react to problems in their childhood in more troubling and traumatic ways than non-HSPs.[27]

This book struck me like a tsunami. For 47 years, I had never understood why I seem to expect so much more from people than they see any reason to give, or why I get upset about things that don't bother other people. I'd never understood why I seemed so fragile or why I can't let go of things that upset me, or why I have always felt so empty and alone. And I had agonized over being unable to understand why I seem to have been so harmed by parents who, at worst, seemed benignly negligent or just narcissistic and insensitive.

Before reading Dr. Aron's book, my only answer to those questions was that I was weak, broken, or not meant to live. I certainly have felt all my life that the world has no place for me. Dr. Aron's book had, for the first time in my life, given me an answer to why I am the way I am. More importantly, her answer did not require me to hate myself or the world around me anymore, including my sister, mother, friends, or clients.

Most importantly, after years of therapy and all the books I'd read and all the therapists and physicians I'd spoken with over the years, I knew that the only way to get better now was to forgive myself and the world around me. For 47 years, I had coped with my inability to understand why I was so different through anger and defiance. I became driven by a visceral hatred of a world that doesn't understand or appreciate me and by thriving in a world designed to destroy me by exploiting its blind spots. I adopted the middle finger as my personal logo—I have several sculptures of middle fingers in my home and often look at them when playing Nirvana on my guitar. Dr. Aron's book gave me a way to try to let go of the hatred and forgive.

Soon after completing Dr. Aron's book, I began reconsidering many troubling events from my past by framing them in the context of these new revelations. Without intending to do so, I began with my sister's failure to react glowingly to my wedding gift, perhaps because of the recency of my email venting about her failure to accept the invitation to my Facebook group about backpacking. More likely, it was because I knew my sister was the most important person to me other than my wife and daughter.

I figured it all out by writing another email to my sister. Without even knowing what I set out to write, I began a follow-up to my email one week earlier confessing my pain from the wedding gift experience. I began by noting that the prior email was one-sided, and that I had not even considered that she had probably kept to herself many things I'd done over the years that hurt her deeply. I also noted that I rarely let her get a word in and never listen to her the way I should. And I acknowledged that this was all wrong, and that it was time to correct it.

I then wrote a detailed moral inventory of everything I could recall having ever done to her that I should not have done and that must have hurt her. I was exhaustive and merciless in my self-examination. I began with how I mistreated her as a child by teaching her not to complain about the bad things I did to her, and how I inappropriately took out anger at my parents on her as a teenager. I addressed the times I called her at night in 1999 while suicidally depressed, then never called her the next day to let her know I was doing better. I confessed to the unfair negative things I'd thought about her as an adult that I likely used as excuses to cope with the pain of her not glowing about the wedding gift, and the pain caused by believing that our intimacy had been a figment of my imagination. I even apologized for not reaching out to her during our eight-year break to express concern when her daughter broke her arm or when her husband—my good friend—had a life-threatening car accident. I acknowledged that all of it was wrong, especially if I was going to guilt trip her about the wedding gift issue that I'd never considered important enough to discuss before. And I apologized.

In an unusual moment of brevity, I titled the email simply, "Acknowledgment." My sister and brother-in-law now call it my Yom Kippur email because of its atonement. I did not expect a response, and I was not sending it to elicit a reaction. I also drew no causal relationship between having read Dr. Aron's book and my decision to send the email. I sent the email because its sentiments needed to be said and the record needed to be set straight. If it had any positive effect on my sister or our relationship, that was only coincidental. I sent the email because I needed to acknowledge everything I'd done to her in order to forgive her and get better.

The morning after I sent my Yom Kippur email to my sister, I stopped thinking about her and resumed obsessing about my out-of-state friend's comment in December about not drinking. I was not inclined to forgive him yet. I instead spent the entire morning becoming more angry by his comment and preparing to finally respond to the email he sent in December apologizing for his drinking comment. I did not plan to write him another Yom Kippur email.

When I finally sat down to write that email, I had a good idea of what I would say. To my credit, I did begin by thanking him for his friendship over the years, and even acknowledged that he may not have meant to hurt my feelings and could fairly accuse me of being overly sensitive. I then recounted the reasons I had been so sensitive, including my mother's harmful decision to send me to rehab directly from hospitalization for suicidal depression and the awful Florida Bar contract that I was forced to endure as a result. I also reminded him that he had previously acknowledged that I should never have been sent to rehab because I'm not an alcoholic. I then recited a list of terrible things that have happened to me since he made his drinking comment in December and implied that his comment caused those terrible things. I closed by telling him that although I valued his friendship, we've grown apart and his values no longer make him compatible with me. And I asked him to never contact me again.

But I didn't click send on that email.

I have always considered myself a writer, and I love to read what I write, not only to edit and polish, but because I relish reading the things I write. I read and re-read my writing the way a beauty queen spends hours brushing her hair. She does it not because it's necessary, but because nothing makes her happier than looking at her hair in the mirror. I continued to fine tune and wordsmith the email I prepared for my out-of-state friend until I thought it was good enough. But as I often do with important motions or legal memoranda, once I got it into its final form, I took a five-minute break to clear my thoughts before giving it one more polishing and pressing send.

During that five-minute break, I posed a hypothetical to myself: What would the email look like if I changed only the ending, and this time did *not* end the relationship? At that moment, I did not *want* to send a conciliatory email allowing the friendship to survive; I was simply interested academically in what an alternative email would look and sound like. In other words, the beauty queen wanted to see how her hair would look if she combed it to the other side, only because she delights in playing with her hair. I returned to my computer and began a new draft of the same email with a different ending.

As with my Yom Kippur email to my sister, I had no idea what I would say when I began writing. For three straight months, I had never even considered continuing the friendship; I had only refrained from communicating with my friends to avoid further embarrassment. I expected those friendships to starve to death from inattention like most friendships do. But as I began typing, the words began to pour out. And although I had never thought about them before, I knew each word was true the moment I wrote it.

I began by reporting my sabbatical, the reasons for it, and my request that he keep it confidential. I also added that I've begun to suspect I'm getting paranoid. But I added that I'm getting better, and that I did not want him to worry or feel bad.

I then acknowledged that I had been deeply upset by his text about drinking and the negative things that happened shortly thereafter, but I've begun to realize that the negative events that occurred after he made his comment were not caused by him, but instead by the mental health issues that I'm dealing with now. I explained that I had become extremely sensitive to being judged over recent months, and this sensitivity to judgment was making me angry in ways I had trouble controlling. I also confessed that I'd wanted to end the friendship with him ever since he made his comment, but I refrained from reaching out to him to avoid saying things I could not take back. I added that I had even drafted an email to end the friendship with him right before preparing this email and was relieved I hadn't sent it to him.

I then confessed that I had recently become very angry at his wife, even though I could not remember her ever doing anything that justified the amount of anger I felt. I also confessed that I had dreaded coming to the get-together in December because I knew she would be there and feared that she would unfairly scrutinize the things I said or my life decisions. I also suspected that my anger toward his wife was delusional. I recounted how I'd similarly felt intensely angry toward another friend's wife years earlier, but I now like her and cannot recall exactly why I had felt so intensely negative about her. I then suggested that I now believe that I wasn't offended at all by his suggestion that I not drink at the get-together, and that I may have been transferring my apprehension about being around his wife to a more easily confessed wound from his comment about drinking, but I wasn't sure.

I closed by apologizing to his wife if I offended her, and I told him that I planned to keep the blocks on his and my other college friend's phone numbers for the time being until I got better, not because I was afraid of what they would say to me, but because I was afraid of what I'd say to them. I also made clear that I no longer wanted to end our friendship.

After finishing the second email, I had no doubt which of the two emails I would send him.

By now, I was beginning to suspect that my latest emails to my sister and out-of-state friend were proof that the Prozac was finally kicking in. Within hours of drafting the second email to my out-of-state friend, I would confirm this in a frightening way.

My wife arrived home from work shortly after I finished the second email, while I was reveling on our back patio about the progress I'd made coping with my mental health issues since reading Dr. Aron's book. Of the four problems that I had been agonizing over for months, I had taken steps to positively resolve two and knew that I was likely to stop obsessing about them now; I now had only two concerns left to address (the conflict with my clients and the barrel of problems with my mother). But rather than simply tell my wife about the conciliatory email I had now decided to send to my out-of-state friend after almost sending him an email ending the relationship, I decided to confuse my wife unnecessarily after a busy day of work. I presented her with the drafts of both emails and told her to read them, then tell me which email she thought I should send.

I thought it would be obvious which email to send, and I did not expect to get an equivocal response. If I had, I would have skipped the game and avoided the chaos that ensued. But when she walked back out on the patio, I was overly excited, and I had unreasonable expectations about the enthusiastic and instant applause I expected to receive. My wife is just not that kind of person. She is measured and even keeled, and she does not jump up and down with excitement in such moments like a gameshow contestant. On this occasion, she did not immediately communicate any understanding that the conciliatory email was the one I wanted to send, and she did not celebrate my accomplishment with adequate enthusiasm.

In fairness to my wife, I doubt anything she would have said would have been good enough. I would soon come to realize that I was severely overstimulated at that moment. I had read a 250-page book in 48 hours, then made more profound progress in two days dealing with a pair of problems I had long agonized over than I had made in the preceding three months. I was excited, but I was exhausted. I had not slept more than three or four hours in a night for almost three months, except for a handful of nights in a tent. So I was, without knowing it, on the verge of mental collapse. I was also beginning to experience strange physiological symptoms, including waking in the middle of the night in a pool of sweat with my body in a state of high agitation that could not be soothed.

After my wife failed to provide the celebratory positive feedback that I afforded her only a second or two to provide, I detonated. I can't remember exactly how I reacted, but as best I can recall, I exploded simultaneously with anger and inconsolable despair. I meanly asked her rhetorically how she could not realize that I intended to send the conciliatory email. I then burst into tears and sobbed that I was deluding myself by thinking I was getting better, and I would, in fact, never get better. My apocalyptically negative thoughts raced at light speed, and I assume my speech did as well. I was putting on another show for the neighbors. After many minutes going back and forth with my wife between anger and despair, I asked her to go inside and think again about what I was asking and begged her to show me some indication that she understood what I was trying to do.

When she came out, she had sunglasses on, and perhaps because of my terrible vision, I could not see her eyes or her facial expressions behind the glasses. I verbally attacked her for not showing emotion and told her that talking to her with such face coverings was like talking to an alien wearing an opaque helmet. The panic and racing thoughts worsened, and I became more hopeless and despondent. I eventually began sobbing that she was the only person in the world who cared about me enough to attempt to understand me, and if she did not understand me, no one ever would. I meant this sincerely and was terrified.

Eventually I demanded that she return inside again to give me time alone to try to regain control of my emotions. But the moment she left, I felt an uncontrollable need to leave my home and get away from her. I had the good sense not to drive, so I fled my back patio quickly without telling her or taking my phone and walked to a park in our neighborhood. She eventually followed me, and a loud shouting match ensued, with me doing the shouting about how I could not continue living if she would never understand me. I was instantly embarrassed about any neighbors who witnessed my psychotic rantings and added shame to my despair and desperation.

My wife eventually convinced me to return home with her, and the night continued as many of the nights of prior panic attacks had gone, except this time, my wife asked the mother of my daughter's best friend if my daughter could spend the night with her. (I should describe the mother of my daughter's best friend instead as a good friend of mine as well, as she has provided unflinching support and kindness to our family throughout the months since my depression returned.)

As before, I was unable to calm down or even determine what I wanted and needed. As before, I drank to calm my nerves enough to sleep. As before, my wife did not sleep, and I slept perhaps an hour or two. But this time, I woke up in a pool of sweat, having forgotten that I had fallen asleep in my wife's bed, and I didn't recognize her and communicated this in a way that must have frightened her. My mind was trapped in a strait jacket of fear and alarm. Even though I knew my wife loved me, I could not convince myself that she had my best interests in mind. Any time we began speaking to each other, I raved at sprint speed and could not let her get a word in, even at 4:00 in the morning.

By the time the sun rose, my wife was far past her wits' end, and we had both already decided to call my therapist the moment her office opened to report my comments in the park about being afraid to continue living. Despite my best efforts, I could not slow my mind down enough to let my wife respond to questions I was asking.

As a last resort, I suggested a bizarre solution. I stepped out of the room, then sent her a text message proposing that we communicate by typing detailed messages to each other on my computer. My theory was that I would type any questions or comments I had while she was in the other room, and when I was done, I would gesture to her that I was done. Then I would leave, and she would read what I wrote and type out her own answers, questions, and comments, then come get me when she was ready for me to respond. This allowed her to finally ask what she needed to ask without interruption.

In my first typed message, I told her that I was afraid of her, and I did not trust or believe anything she was telling me. I explained that I knew that was absurd, but for reasons I did not understand and could not control, it was true. But I added that I think it might get better if I could just calm down, and I suspected that if we continued to communicate through writing rather than talking, I could calm down enough to finally start talking again. But I told her that it was critical that she understood, otherwise there was no hope of getting me to calm down enough to communicate. She responded by typing that she understood and that she loved me and would do whatever was needed to help me get better.

By 8:30 in the morning, I had calmed down enough to apologize and speak with her again in person, and by 9:00, I was calm enough to join her call with my therapist and assure my therapist that I was not suicidal, but had just become scared and expressed a desire to die because it was the only way I thought I could relieve the pain I was experiencing. We agreed that I would not be hospitalized, but that if anything worse happened before my next appointment, we would call her immediately. My wife and I then spent the rest of the day recovering from the panic attack, which was the worst I had experienced this century.

That panic attack began on a Thursday and ended on the Friday before my next appointment with my therapist the following Monday. No more panic attacks followed, but I continued to experience alarming physiological symptoms that weekend that I could not control. I could now sleep no more than two hours at a time, and when I woke up drenched in sweat, I was frightened and could not calm down for hours. Then during the day, I began experiencing radical mood swings during which, without warning, I became intensely agitated and needed to avoid contact with my wife and daughter for fear of lashing out at them. When these mood swings occurred at night, I had to immerse myself in bright lights and lie down on the floor of my bathroom to calm down. The task was made more difficult by my wife's preference for soft white light bulbs, which I called "depression lights." I went to Home Depot, purchased extra bright white light bulbs, and replaced all the soft white bulbs as soon as I got home. My wife also bought a special ultra bright lamp that I could turn on from my bed by using a remote control. Although I needed a television to sleep and calm down, I could no longer watch any commercials and had to limit myself to a handful of PBS documentaries on demand.

By the time Monday morning arrived, I strongly suspected that these new symptoms had to be related to the Prozac finally taking effect, and we called my psychiatrist and set a zoom appointment for the next morning. We were scheduled to fly to Arizona in five days and I feared what I might do at a crowded airport or on a plane if the symptoms arose there. Even if I cancelled the trip to Arizona, I did not know how much longer I could live with these new symptoms. My psychiatrist understood what was happening and prescribed a second mood stabilizing medication and offered me the hope that it would take effect quickly. He also recommended adjustments to my diet and behavior that could abate the new symptoms.

It all worked out. The scary new symptoms began waning immediately after I began taking the second medication, and when those symptoms occurred again, they were less intense and more easily controlled. I suspect my wife struggled with whether to cancel our trip to Arizona, but I knew it was worth the risk to go. We planned to spend most of the trip hiking or touring museums, national parks, and the University of Arizona. Travel and hiking had always soothed me and helped me deal with my demons. I also knew that canceling the trip would be traumatic for my daughter, and she had already been through too much and needed some happy times. God love her—my wife had faith in me, my medications, and the care I was receiving, much of which she was providing. We therefore took the spring break trip as scheduled.

Coffee Pot Rock in Sedona, Arizona, March 20, 2024.

CHAPTER TEN

Returning to Neverland

When we got on our flight to Phoenix for our spring break trip to Arizona, my wife and I were hoping for the best but preparing for the worst. We had planned the trip and booked our accommodations months before my depression returned, so we were glad to not have to cancel our flights and the Vrbo we booked in Sedona and lose what we had already spent on them. But we were only eight days removed from my worst panic attack in 20 years, and only three days past scary physiological symptoms that left me uncontrollably irritable and alarmed when overstimulated; we knew we were in for some serious stimulation. The meds I had begun taking three days earlier were clearly starting to work. We also knew that we could restructure our trip to accommodate the latest curveballs in my mental health.

Step one was to find a new place to stay in Tucson. We were to visit Tucson for the first weekend and had planned to stay with the family of a friend of mine from that law school in Virginia, and we would then drive north to Sedona and stay at a rental house for the rest of the week near the head of a popular trail. Ironically, the law school friend was one of the few people who knew about my suicidal depression in 1999, so I felt comfortable warning him about my latest issues. But I did not want to expose his wife or their son to a raving panic attack, so we politely let them know that we had decided to book a Vrbo closer to downtown Tucson, which was fine with them.

We had not made plans about what we would do with them before we left, but when they proposed that we spend a relaxing Saturday afternoon and evening on their back patio and pool with their friendly Great Dane and precocious son, we were relieved to have a stress-free day. We ended up having a great, relaxing time with them that helped me heal, especially after we watched a long sunset over the Tucson Mountains that rivaled what I had seen on the trail in Florida. We even enjoyed a rare sighting of an Arizona wildcat that popped by our friends' patio to have a drink from their pool.

Tucson allowed me to reset and get off to a good start. I had a scare the morning after we arrived when I began experiencing the physiological symptoms that the new meds were meant to address, but my wife figured out that I had forgotten to take my medications the night before when I returned to our rental home exhausted from the flight. Minutes after I wolfed down my overdue pills, I began feeling better and felt better the rest of the weekend. On Sunday, we had our first hike of the trip at Saguaro National Park before returning to have dinner again with our friends. Mission accomplished at Tucson.

The second half of the trip to Sedona was a wonderful time of healing for all of us. We had booked a house less than a mile from the head of a trail that was so popular that hikers were required to park at a lot one and a half miles away and either walk or take a bus to the trailhead, so we effectively had special access to the Soldiers Pass trail. Our pretty, spacious house had patios in the front and back with views of Sedona's breathtaking rock formations, along with a hot tub in the backyard. Being unable to sleep past 5 a.m. is much easier when your bed faces the eastern sunrise through sliding glass doors, and you have a Zen Garden to enjoy your morning coffee while staring at Coffee Pot Rock.

Our time in Sedona was also somewhat of an extension of my backpacking odyssey in Florida. We spent four full days in Sedona, and for three of them, we hiked in the morning before the trails became busy, then made a bee line home, grabbed a beer or a soda, ripped off our boots, jumped into the hot tub, and drew straws for who would bring lunch out. We then relaxed the rest of the afternoon while watching hikers walk by our house to and from Soldiers Pass while sipping beverages on our patio. I even brought my tent and sleeping bag and slept in the backyard one night, hours after we saw a pair of *javelina* walk through (Peccaries, or javelina *en Español*, are omnivorous mammals that are related to pigs and look similar to the hogs we see in Florida but are classified in their own family. We were also warned by our friends in Tucson that they can be dangerous and even attacked a neighbor and his dogs while he was jogging in his neighborhood.)

My time at Sedona was a therapeutic respite from the pain I had experienced in the preceding three months. We hiked 21 miles during those three days, twice on trails that we walked to from our house. Although I was more fit for the hills and the distance than my girls because of my

Boynton Canyon Trail in Sedona, Arizona, March 21, 2024.

February backpacking, they both stayed with me pace for pace through sweat and foot soreness. They certainly managed the cliffs better than me, as heights and I are not on speaking terms. Our early starts meant that trails notorious for being crowded were largely empty during the first halves of our hikes. Returning home and jumping into a muscle-soothing outdoor bathtub while sipping a cold beer was just what the doctor ordered.

I was still only managing three hours of sleep a night, but I was adapting to functioning on only three hours of light non-REM sleep as I had in the past. Because of the meds, I also agonized less when I couldn't fall back to sleep and instead stared through my open shades at the southwestern stars. I was also finally able to get myself to take one-hour afternoon cat naps, and my girls let me sleep in peace on the living room couch every afternoon and then gently woke me up in time to arrive early and stress-free to downtown Sedona for our dinner reservations. You would be surprised how much just one extra hour of sleep can help your mood and outlook on life.

The best part of the trip was being able to hike with my wife and daughter. I could not share any of the backpacking adventures described in this book with them because camping is not their thing. My daughter is a Swiftie who loves to entertain and enjoys soccer, but she's never once asked to sleep in a tent, and I will not be surprised if she never gets the urge. My wife backpacked ages ago in Colorado with her sister, but as much fun as she had there, she did not enjoy the inconveniences of sleeping on the ground. But my girls and I have always hiked together. With family that lives in Montana

Hiking at Soldiers Pass Trail in Sedona, Arizona, March 19, 2024.

and Washington, we've hiked at seven different national parks, including Yellowstone, Glacier, and Mount Rainier.

My girls therefore had no problem doing training hikes with me in the weeks leading up to our trip and were prepared for distances of longer than four miles. I still expected to break free for extra mileage occasionally given my recent backpacking. But my girls stayed with me stride for stride, climbing up switchbacks, clinging to canyon walls, and searching for cairns and blazes on rock formations. My sixth grader could have been forgiven for complaining, especially on the long rolling uphill climbs, but she was all smiles and earned an A for attitude. My wife was, as usual, the calm, supportive team leader who preserved our memories with well-shot photos and videos. She's a better Spielberg than me.

Sedona is a special place. There are hundreds of miles of trails, from famous routes like Soldiers Pass that are must-sees for anyone willing to step out of the pink jeep to small pieces of heaven kept secret by locals. They all have breathtaking views of giant monoliths painted in the morning and evening by pink and orange rays of sun. You do not have to hike to enjoy Sedona, but it certainly makes the experience more immersive. We will never forget slowly descending through the low grasses and shrubs of Brins Mesa after our hardest climb up the nearby pass, leaving all signs of civilization behind and below. Or slowly ascending through the Boynton Canyon as its vertical walls inched closer like the jaws of a giant trash compactor, as monumental ponderosa pine stood guard to save our escape route to the morning sun. Or eating lunch panting on cliffs beside ancient cave dwellings among hordes of other tourists with sweat-stained hats and wide grins tattooed on their chins.

In the months since taking my first steps into the world of solo backpacking, I've come to realize how my time in joyful isolation in the forests and prairies near my home helped heal my depression and the bad memories from my childhood and early adulthood. During those hikes with my girls in Sedona and Saguaro, I was fully aware of being healed by each step and each smile and hug I shared with my wife and daughter. Moments like those can never be missed.

There were a few scary moments during the trip. About an hour before boarding the flight home to Orlando, I became overstimulated and irrationally impatient with my wife, and I had to find a quiet place away from other travelers, put in my earbuds, and blast Nirvana at full volume to calm down. Nevertheless, I boarded the plane, apologized to my girls, and did not ruin the flight. There may have been another close call or two as well, but the trip was otherwise exactly what I needed to start getting better.

After we returned from Arizona, I felt considerably improved, and I felt intuitively that the time may be approaching for me to end my sabbatical and return to work. I finally felt better physically, and my wife was seeing changes in my behavior. I was less agitated and seemed to be brooding less. I was also hungry to practice law again and to help support my family. I missed writing, I missed analyzing cases, and I even missed my clients, at least the ones who were receptive to my advice. I also missed my team—the two assistants who were scrambling to assist attorneys asked to cover my cases and who I knew were looking forward to my return.

I didn't want to take any chances though, and after sharing my newfound peace with my therapist, we agreed that I would wait for one more week to decide whether and when to return to work. If I made it to Friday without any significant incident or panic attack, I would inform my boss about my intention to return to work and pick a date.

I did not yet have pleasant feelings when thinking about the client conflict that had triggered my sabbatical, and I was still reluctant to think about the way I was treated or how I would react if treated that way again. But I preferred to build up to such strength while reactivating my mental muscles litigating, rather than waiting for the moment when life was somehow perfect to begin practicing law again. I also doubted that I could fully recover without first returning to work.

When Friday arrived and I had still not had any setbacks, I reached out to my boss and agreed with him that I would return to work two weeks later, on April 15th.

I also yearned to return to the trail as soon as possible. Having had so much fun in February, I was not ready to wait nine months to do it again, and I still had two weeks until I had to say goodbye to the trail until next season. With the new medication and a three-week break from backpacking, I did not want to return with too difficult a challenge—I chose to go somewhere familiar.

I had previously chosen the Buster Island Loop when making my first trip to Lake Kissimmee State Park, and it only seemed logical to refresh my body to backpacking by now doing the 6.5-mile North Loop. It was more heavily forested than the Buster Island Loop, which I suspected might help with the warmer afternoon heat on the hike in. With spring break for most local schools having ended the week before, reservations were plentiful, and I was able to book the primitive campsite for that Saturday. Although we had friends coming to visit us Sunday afternoon, I knew I could hike out early enough to arrive home in time to shower before our guests came. I booked the campsite and packed my gear immediately. For those scoring at home, I spent both Valentine's Day and Easter at Lake Kissimmee State Park.

I cannot overstate how great it felt to be back home on the trail. I didn't quite feel that way on the hike in, as the day was hot and windless, and several stretches of the trail had recently been burned and therefore offered little shade. I also was nearly run over on the hikers only trail by an elderly couple driving a golf cart who seemed to think they had the right of way. But I became instantly cool and euphoric as soon as I reached the campsite and ripped off my backpack. I was tempted to strip immediately, but instead spent my first few minutes lying atop the picnic table and telling the live oaks and pine trees how much I had missed them.

The real fun began when I left two hours before sunset to explore. My options were limited as I had hiked this trail before and was not dying to go further down or up the North

Loop again. But a few hundred yards from my campsite, the trail was crossed by a grassy jeep road that led deeper into the park and eventually to one of the lakes abutting Buster Island. I had high hopes that I might see wildlife, and it was a good sign when I spooked a deer right after leaving my campsite.

The jeep road rambled deeper into a forest of palmetto and pine, and as the sugar sand thickened, it was replaced by grasses; I became less aware that I was on a road rather than a trail. I certainly did not get the impression that a vehicle had been there recently. As the sun began to fall lower on the horizon, my anticipation of seeing deer rose. But my excitement slowly began morphing into caution as the brush beside the road became thicker, the grass on the road became taller, and the water table rose. I suspected I may not make it to within sight of the lake without risking an encounter with an alligator, and my senses immediately activated to high alert while scanning the trail for rattlesnakes.

But I was in for a far better treat. About one mile down the jeep road, as I rounded a corner and scanned past a group of low trees and bushes, I saw three dark knee-high ovals lined up across the trail about 30 yards in front of me. I found wild hogs.

The wild pigs that can be found virtually everywhere in Florida are not a native species, but instead the descendants of those brought to Florida by Spanish and other European explorers on their ships as a food source. They are voracious, non-picky eaters who often leave large basketball-size holes on the trail that can be annoying to backpackers' ankles and that lead those new to hiking to wonder how a small backhoe

Above: Deer along the North Loop, Lake Kissimmee State Park, March 31, 2024. Right: Wild hogs near the North Loop, Lake Kissimmee State Park, March 30, 2024.

made it so far into the wilderness. They also have sharp tusks and little fear and should be treated with respect. When I was a Boy Scout, my friends and I dug traps with sharpened palmetto spears covered by palmetto fronds on game trails near our campsites to attempt to catch them (the only thing we ever trapped was one of our adult leaders). I also recall one night when we chose to sleep under the stars in hammocks and used lighters and aerosol bug spray as blow torches to defend ourselves from wild boar who darted through our campsite at night looking for crumbs and trash. We used blow torches more than once, but not on any animals other than each other.

Wild hogs are beautiful, and I had not seen many mammals during my trips in February, particularly from close range. So being a son of my generation, I approached with my cell phone out and set for video, and Spielberg began framing his shots for the Facebook group.

When I got about 20 yards from the adult hogs (fortunately downwind), I saw a piglet hopping through the grass halfway between me and its likely parents. Circumstances had instantly changed. Like most animals, hogs are known to aggressively protect their young. They charge first and ask questions later. I immediately realized that if I got any closer, I might get charged, and having never wrestled a wild animal or even gotten into a fight in grade school, I did not like my odds of winning that battle. I also knew that wild animals typically have better senses of smell and hearing than me, being more accustomed than most humans to living their entire lives watching their backs for things that want to eat them.

I immediately froze and uncontrollably passed a lot of gas. I continued watching every move of each animal, praying that the piglet would not see me and squeal an alarm. The piglet was oblivious, as it was immersed in rambunctious play in the grasses like a typical toddler, nipping at grasses, toying with them, then losing interest, rolling on its back, and becoming fascinated with some part of its own body. The big boys were still focused on eating and were not helicopter parents. Like the parents of most toddlers, they were enjoying a few minutes of peace while they grabbed something to eat.

Spielberg therefore came back on the set, and he paged the douchey easy listening DJ to narrate. Every now and then I inched closer to offset the low budget zoom function on my phone's video camera. The hogs still appear tiny in the dailies. But Spielberg got at least some footage to prove he wasn't making the story up.

I then put my phone in my pocket and decided to enjoy the moment and forget about bragging on social media about what I saw. I stood watching these beautiful, smelly animals graze as the sun slowly inched down between the trees behind them. I completely forgot about the possibility that I might be standing too close to an easily surprised poisonous snake, and instead stood in the grass watching the hogs for 15 minutes while taking occasional drags on my nicotine vape and watching the early evening clouds roll by. I was home again.

When I finally hiked back, I saw several more deer close to my campsite. It would have been nice if I had thought ahead and brought a jacket to cover my bright orange dri-fit shirt. As all hunters know, deer see orange clearly, and when a deer that hasn't been fed by jerks sees someone wearing orange, it usually turns around and runs away before you can snap a selfie with it. So these guys didn't stick around, but at least I got my fill of bouncing deer butt for the evening.

Getting back to camp reminded me of everything I had missed about backpacking, and I stuck to the script. I made another freeze-dried dinner as the sun set, then enjoyed it from atop my picnic table while seated on the camp stool to get elevated views of the sun setting around my campsite. I had now developed a solid routine for coordinating cleaning myself with beginning the campfire. I built my fire and prepared the kindling for instant ignition, then pulled out my yuppie shower wipe and the clean clothes to put on as soon as mosquitoes started nipping my unmentionables. I then stripped, wiped the dirt off my legs and arms with the inside of my sweaty socks, lathered with the yuppie wipe, then immediately lit the fire and dangled my trailer hitch jewelry above the rising smoke, just in case the humidity put the fire out too quickly for a thorough smoking. The fire lasted for more than 2 hours, and so did my public nudity. My mind rambled with laughter like a puppy playing with a new toy.

The stars were once again bright and plentiful, and I was serenaded by mooing cows from a nearby ranch as I gazed at the night sky, which made for an amusing soundtrack amidst the hooting of my owls. I also heard the occasional boat go by in the distance on Lake Kissimmee. I even received a bonus to remind me that I was a Central Floridian when I saw an arching orange glow in the distance to the east. I immediately recognized that it was a rocket launching from Cape Canaveral—we routinely see rocket launches from our

*Campfire at North Loop campsite at Lake Kissimmee State Park,
March 30, 2024.*

home in Winter Garden further east. Alas, my night was capped with fireworks to celebrate my imminent return to work.

I went to bed around midnight and slept, once again, an hour or two more than I could yet at home, even though I was more interested in watching stars and the sunrise. When I woke an hour before dawn, I knew I had too short a hike out but also a tight schedule. I decided to break camp early and add three miles to the end of my hike by doing most of the Gobbler Ridge Loop Trail again, increasing the distance for my morning hike to 5 miles. My fun with my four-legged neighbors would soon resume.

Spring mornings in Central Florida are a great time to see deer. I had become enamored years earlier with Wekiwa Springs State Park because of how many deer I saw when hiking on its six-mile Volksmarch Trail in early mornings. I even bought an annual pass to obtain after-hours access so I could begin those hikes before dawn. I got a relatively late start on the North Loop when I left that morning at 8:30, but apparently the deer were also lagging behind from the recent time change because they were out in full force.

After seeing several deer off the trail early in my hike out, I came upon three more while crossing the park's main road with less than a mile to go before reaching the Gobbler Ridge. One was less than 10 yards to my left along the road, and two others were on the far side of the road beside the trail. I alerted Spielberg and began rolling film, and I was glad to not be wearing orange this time. As I calmly and quietly said good morning and began crossing the road, one of the deer on the far side stared, came closer, and then jumped further into the palmettos. But the other two were unphased, even after I walked by the one closest to the trail at less than 2 feet of distance. I was clearly not the first person they'd seen that week, and it was breakfast time, so they were not inclined to pay attention to me. My inner hippie had been placated.

As I hiked later down the Gobbler Ridge trail, I felt a percussive "swoosh" above my head and looked ahead to see a hawk land on a branch in front of me and stare with disdain. I had clearly disrupted its morning routine, and it was letting me know that it was still quiet time in the forest. My apologies, my friend. Five minutes later, I saw a turkey cross the trail about ten yards ahead, but I was not able to follow where it went as it rambled awkwardly past the live oaks. Best of all, when I went back to the bench beside Lake Kissimmee to finish my trail mix before heading home, I saw a large bald eagle glide by above the beach. I guess the rangers at Lake Kissimmee have these animals well-trained for the animal show.

It took more than a little bit of willpower to leave the park in time to arrive before our friends came to visit. During the drive home, I could think about nothing but the calendar and where I would go next before leaving Neverland and returning to the real world two weeks later.

CHAPTER ELEVEN

The Ecstasy and the Agony

W hen I returned home from my second trip to Lake Kissimmee State Park, I knew the clock was ticking. I had only 15 days until I was to return to work, but I absolutely *had* to continue backpacking while I could. Given my pace of one trip per week in February, I hoped I could do two more trips rather than just one, but the weather had become hotter, and I wasn't sure I could sleep in the warmer weather. It would therefore now be more critical than ever to surf weather windows. I might also need to shorten the break between trips, which I thought (incorrectly) might tax my middle-aged body.

One thing was certain: I was no longer going to consider any option that did not include the Florida Trail. The taste generated by the Florida Trail when hiking in the Withlacoochee State Forest was more than a little bit addictive. I knew my best chance of finding not just a beautiful campsite, but also a beautiful trail ideal for hiking, was to follow the Florida Trail. I also no longer needed the safety and security of a state park. I was ready for a trail meant only for backpackers in a wild place devoid of people, ideally far away from cars and other signs of civilization.

I also wanted to stay close to home if possible, and the west branch of the Florida Trail ran not far from my house. I knew that loop trails connecting to the Florida Trail were rare and most were too long for a one-nighter, so I had to now consider out-and-back hikes rather than loops, but I did not mind. Many backpackers dislike out-and-back trips because they don't want to see the same trail twice. But in my experience, a trail looks different when walking in reverse direction, especially when the weight of a backpack keeps you from fully appreciating the scenery as much as you might like on the hike in.

In preparing for my hikes, I also knew I had to be ready to do greater distances. The furthest I had thus far hiked in with the full 40ish pounds of weight was 5.1 miles at the Croom Tract. But campsites are typically spaced more than five miles apart on the Florida Trail, so I knew I needed to be ready to hike further with gear—and in greater heat. I was therefore going to officially be challenging myself. But after carrying more than 20 pounds day after day on Sedona's boulders with altitude and elevation, I was confident I could handle the greater distance if I avoided weather that was too hot.

What followed were the two hardest but most satisfying trips of my first backpacking season. Indeed, the last trip was my crucible and the only trip that made me feel like a real backpacker who could handle adversity. The first trip constituted perhaps my most exhilarating 24 hours outdoors.

My first weather window arrived on the Thursday and Friday of the second-to-last week of my sabbatical, and after considering options further away, I settled on an option barely an hour away from my home, in the West Tract of the Green Swamp.

The Green Swamp sits halfway between Orlando and the Croom Tract of the Withlacoochee Forest near Brooksville where I'd hiked in February. More of a forest than a swamp, the Green Swamp is a slightly elevated portion of Central Florida comprising thousands of acres of pristine forest and wetlands that serve as the headwaters for four of Florida's major rivers, the Withlacoochee, Hillsborough, Ocklawaha, and Peace. It is managed by the Southwest Florida Water Management District and is used by hikers, hunters, Boy Scouts, horse riders, and those riding ATVs (although fortunately not many), so its campsites are free but still need to be reserved. Thirty miles of the Florida Trail run through the East and West Tracts of the Green Swamp, which are separated by the north-south State Road 471. After overcoming an initial fear that mosquitoes would abound in anything labeled a *swamp*, I elected to follow the recommendation from one of my guidebooks and planned a trip from the McNeil trailhead at the eastern border of the West Tract north and west to the Concession Stand backcountry campsite.

This trip promised to challenge me. The campsite I chose was 7.5 miles from the trailhead, so I would be hiking a minimum of 15 miles in 24 hours and almost fifty percent more miles on the hike in than during on any prior trip.

Florida National Scenic Trail at the Green Swamp, West Tract, April 5, 2024.

I was also hiking in hotter weather—projected in the high 70s. Even so, it was still less than what I had at the most recent trip to Lake Kissimmee, but I would still be hiking in the peak heat of the late afternoon. There would be no park rangers. I'd pull off to an empty grass parking lot on the side of a road otherwise surrounded by nothing but forest for miles in every direction, and if I had any trouble, I'd have to either take care of myself or wait a long time for help. So I had to plan much better by printing my own maps and using colored highlighters and the Florida Trail Guide to identify milestones and side trails (translation: potential wrong turns to avoid). Because of the distances and heat, I took more water and food.

Within moments of beginning my hike in around 2:00 in the afternoon, I knew I had made the right decision. I was immediately immersed in a desolate, quiet forest of tall pines that reminded me of the Ewok planet from *Return of the Jedi*. The trail was perfect in every way. It wasn't just that it was a narrow, winding hikers only trail with barely enough width to allow hikers to pass each other in opposite directions while one stood to the side. The walking surface was also perfect. Gone were the days of hiking in loose sugar sand sifted and churned by mountain bike and jeep tires. Now I was on a firm, soft bed of soil topped by pine needles.

The greatest effort was clearly made by the Florida Trail Association to avoid roads, even if it meant carving winding trails hidden beside roads. The trail is also immaculately maintained by the FTA. You almost never struggle to find blazes or see a walking surface, and the only obstacles are occasional recently fallen trees or holes rooted out by hogs.

This trail is also *empty*. I saw no one on the trail except when passing the more popular Gator Hole campsite less than two miles from the trailhead at the end of my hike out. I could have walked naked the whole hike in from trailhead to campsite without having to feel bashful. This was the isolation I was looking for.

The terrain also varied considerably and kept me entertained while my mind and legs ignored the miles I was logging. After initially winding through the pine forest, the trail broke out temporarily into a cypress flat with occasional ponds before reaching the large and relatively open but shaded Gator Hole campsite. This was followed shortly thereafter by the Gator Hole itself, a crystal-clear pond with no gators yet but plenty of fish and birds. The trail then ascended slightly into more hilly and densely vegetated terrain, before passing through a slightly mucky section near a grassy jeep road—one of those sections where the FTA had carved out parallel scenic trails. I didn't even take my first drink of water until more than 4 miles into the hike, and any fatigue was buried by endorphin-fueled adrenaline cooled by breezy spring winds.

I had my failure for the trip somewhere between four and five miles into my 7.5-mile hike in, and it was a big, fat rookie mistake. I mentioned earlier that it took me some time to learn that two stacked blazes signal the approach of a junction, and in practical terms mean, "Hey stupid, stay alert and look for blazes to make sure you're still on the trail." Without fully appreciating it, I reached an important point of the Florida Trail where the trail turned due north after ranging west and northwest for several miles. I knew that the turn north happened at a point where the Florida Trail briefly joined the grassy road that I'd been hiking beside, then turned back into the forest and left the grassy road for good, with the grassy road continuing to roll west-northwest. I suspected before reaching that point that I might be on that grassy road for some time.

I was mistaken and it took me longer than it should have to realize my mistake. It was at least 15 minutes before I finally thought, *Gee, it's been a while since I've seen a blaze.* I now blame this on my poor vision—I would finally make a long overdue appointment to get glasses shortly after returning from this trip.

I had two choices. I could have turned around and retraced my steps until I saw the orange blazes and then found the correct trail. But having by now hiked at least 5 miles, I was reluctant to add more miles unnecessarily. Alternatively, my maps seemed to indicate that the road I was on ran roughly parallel to the Florida Trail, albeit more west, and eventually dead-ended onto the only crushed stone road in the area, which the Florida Trail also crossed some distance east. So if I continued walking down this road, I could just turn east once I hit the forest road and then keep my eyes peeled for orange blazes where the Florida Trail crossed.

I chose the latter option, and I did eventually find the Florida Trail to my great relief, but not before adding 1.5 miles to my hike in, most of which was on unshaded roads rather than the shady forested trail. If I wanted a challenge, I gave myself one. My hike in with a 40-pound backpack ended up being 9 miles. It did not surprise me that I also had my first blister of the season after this hike.

As a just punishment, I also hit the sandiest and hilliest terrain during that last 1.5 miles after I finally relocated the Florida Trail, but I was fully hydrated, relieved, and very motivated to reach camp and strip off my backpack and T-shirt. When I finally reached the Concession Stand campsite, I immediately could tell that the stress and extra miles were all to be rewarded.

The Concession Stand campsite sits halfway down the crest of a west-facing sandhill and above a gorgeous pond blanketed on its far side by majestic pine trees. A short trail connects the campsite to the Florida Trail on the ridge of the sandhill, which continues west and passes the pond on the hiker's right. This hilltop provides epic views of sunsets over the pond, sunrises over hills to the east, and stars above the pines after dark.

The campsite itself has everything. There's a small but well-maintained fire ring (no cigarette butts), a solid picnic table, live oaks for shade and tall pines for added beauty, small tent spots surrounded by palmettos near the fire ring, and even a sturdy permanent bench beside the fire pit. A thoughtful FTA member had even left a full bottle of water and a first aid kit under the picnic table, along with a solar powered light that helped guide me to my bear bag line at night. Having forgotten my moleskin, I was glad to be able to tear a small cube from the first aid kit left there for my benefit by the FTA.

It did not take that much extra energy to quickly set up camp, although I wasted time and calories fruitlessly trying to throw my bear bag line 25 feet above the trail across the bough of a longleaf pine. I eventually settled for a much easier low hanging live oak bough, but I asked for trouble by hanging the bag only seven feet off the forest floor. I could have awakened to a black bear playing tether ball with my breakfast, but fortunately no bears stopped by my campsite that night.

After hanging my bear bag, I collapsed with fatigue onto the bench beside the fire pit and stared at a tall pine beside my picnic table while sipping water and munching trail mix. But being the restless guy I am, I eventually decided to sunset hike again. It took little coaxing to convince me to go further up the Florida Trail, as I suspected I would like what I saw.

I did, as I enjoyed some of the most beautiful trails I'd seen all season during that sunset hike. Having left after 5:00 p.m. and wanting to eat before sunset, I planned initially to hike only one mile further down the trail, but after being smitten by what I saw, I had to force myself to turn around 2 miles down the trail to avoid getting lost in the forest at night. The first mile was rolling sandhills, comparable to my hike out at the Croom Tract several weeks earlier but trading the morning fog for falling sun. Then almost without warning, the trail sucked you from the open hills into a forest so thick that I sang the opening line from Guns N' Roses' "Welcome to the Jungle" in the douchey video Spielberg shot while hiking through this stretch on the way back to camp. The little boy racing through the forest an hour before nightfall forgot all about depression, returning to work, or even the fact that he had already hiked ten miles. It took a considerable amount of self-control to return to camp in time for the sunset.

Campfire at Tower West campsite, at the Osceola National Forest,
April 8, 2024.

Naturally, dinner and the sunset were even better than the hike. I had brought one of my favorite freeze-dried dinners, and when I finally finished preparing it at the campsite when the sun fell below the horizon, I scampered up the connector trail with my camp stool and dinner and savored every morsel while I watched the sky darken and listened to the crickets chirp. I had enjoyed many dinners over the past three months on the trail, but this was the best. The sky was clear, the air was cool, the mosquitoes were somewhere else, and my mind kept replaying mile after mile of the hike in and the sunset hike. This was a productive use of an obsessive mind.

The campfire was tricky. The Florida humidity had arrived, so the fire did not last long and took some effort. Fortunately, I had perfected my yuppie shower routine. After preparing the wood and clothes and toiletries, I lit my fire after stripping and then alternated between wiping my sweaty loins with the shampooed wipe and manhandling embers with my fire stick, like a Benihana chef juggling eight meals frying at once.

I was adequately smoked by the time the fire went out for good before 10:00, but that was no reason to put on clothes, and it was certainly no reason to go to bed. The sky was clear, and the owls were louder than ever, and although I could not see the stars that well through the live oak and longleaf pine boughs surrounding my firepit and picnic table, I could see them perfectly from the crest of the hill where I ate dinner. Rising above most of the treetops, the hill was also far enough away from Orlando, Tampa, and their theme parks that their lights were below the horizon. The hundreds of stars were the brightest of any of my trips.

The best surprise was when I woke, as usual, an hour before dawn. Because of the intimacy of my camp, I was able to see a clear view of the sky only by lying on my stomach and looking west through the mesh door of my tent. But 30 minutes after I awoke, I saw an orange and yellow fireball streak from east to west across the still dark sky. I had just seen my first meteor.

This was another morning to not rush, particularly since I thought it could be my last morning at camp for the season. I took my oatmeal with M&Ms and jet fuel coffee back up to the crest of the hill and stayed longer than needed while watching the sunrise, knowing that my car was somewhere in the distance. I also took my time taking down my tent and packing my backpack. I enjoyed every minute I could spare before realizing that the day was only going to get hotter.

The hike out was cooler and more pleasant than the hike in (I even needed gloves for the first mile or two), and because I knew what was coming, I knew when to cue Spielberg and the douchey DJ for good trail footage. I found the turn that I had missed the day before and gagged at my incompetence. But that didn't stop me from missing a few more turns at other junctions and adding an extra half mile to my hike out. But even when I had hiked six miles and saw campers at the Gator Hole campsite, I was still full of smiles and probably annoyed the older gentlemen I passed at camp with my Howdy Doody positivity.

When I reached the car, I felt more energy than I had at the end of any trip thus far, but that quickly evaporated as I began munching on mozzarella sticks and sliced turkey pepperoni while sitting shirtless beneath the rear door of my car. I reclined against my backpack, sipped water, gazed at the surrounding forest, and beamed from ear to ear. I stayed for at least 30 minutes. If this was the way my backpacking season was to end, I had done it the right way.

But that was not the end of my backpacking odyssey, and with eleven days left until my return to the real world, I was committed to taking one more trip. The only remaining cold front in the next ten days was to be the following Monday, and it was not going to be as cool as it was during my dream trip to the Green Swamp. Forecasts in regions crossed by the western leg of the Florida Trail were projected to be particularly warm.

So I looked north—far north, almost all the way to the state line with Georgia. Although I considered the Ocala National Forest, the birthplace of the Florida Trail that includes the first legs of the trail created by the Florida Trail Association, I was deterred by the distance and warnings in several guidebooks that cars are occasionally broken into when left overnight at ungated parking areas near trailheads. Stretches further north, lying east of Gainesville where I went to college, were also too far from major interstates for a reasonable drive and would need to be accessed through towns famous for ticketing drivers who miss hidden speed limit signs that drop lawful speeds to 25 miles per hour.

Florida National Scenic Trail at the Osceola National Forest, April 8, 2024.

I ultimately landed on the Osceola National Forest near Lake City, at a stretch of the Florida Trail northwest of the Olustee Battlefield Historic State Park and just north of I-10, the interstate highway connecting Jacksonville to Pensacola and then New Orleans and Houston. Although this was still more than three hours' drive from my home, it was accessible from I-75, an interstate I could drive blindfolded from my years driving to Gainesville and Tallahassee for college and law school. I had hoped that the added distance would provide cooler temperatures. I also looked forward to seeing what I presumed would be a different ecosystem. I even had the added treat of hiking in during an afternoon eclipse.

Had I thought through my plan a bit more, I would have set myself up for a more enjoyable experience. The more popular stretch of the Florida Trail in this area runs north and west from the Ocean Pond Recreational Area to the Turkey Run trailhead, which also passes by the Osceola Shelter, one of the oldest covered shelters along this stretch of the Florida Trail that sits beside a pretty creek. But the distance of this route was not long enough after my successful nine-mile hike in at the Green Swamp, and I decided to instead do a six and a half mile out-and-back from the Turkey Creek trailhead north and west to the West Tower campsite.

As you may recall from my opening lines, this trip proved to be a challenge because of submerged trails, but any pain felt during my last trip of the season was self-inflicted. I not only *should* have known that I was in for particularly wet trails; I actually knew what I was in for. Sandra Friend and John Keatly, the experienced hikers who wrote *The Florida Trail Guide,* also maintain an excellent backpacking website, floridahikes.com, which has a page detailing the specific trail I chose that warns:

> At several points along this path, the road dips down and is filled with tannin-stained water and soft mud. Depending on the season, these can be ankle to knee deep and 50-100 ft. across.
>
> Several of these water obstacles have walk-arounds (some very overgrown) and one has a boardwalk adjacent to the road.
>
> But one or two do not provide any alternative to wading through, so you will get your feet wet.[28]

I read this before I left, so I knew what I was in for. As I recall, I was not worried about wet boots because of my experience during the hike out on Day 3 of my two-nighter at Myakka River State Park. But as many amateur backpackers learn the hard way, you can't teach stupid.

Wet trails ended up not being the only challenge on my trip to Osceola National Forest. This last trip seemed to throw as much at me as I could handle, to see how much I really enjoyed backpacking and whether I wanted to return to my nerfy life as a desk jockey next season. As it turned out, any troubles I experienced on my last trip of the season did nothing but make me want to return to the trail even more the next season.

Even from the start, there were disconcerting signs. The trail began with a short 0.2-mile sprint through forest before reaching the first of the flooded roads, but the forest near the trailhead had been recently burned, so the pretty forest that I had become so infatuated with was temporarily out of service. I also noticed the second I opened my car door that I would not be alone on the trail. Gnats surrounded my face, and although they never bit, they attacked my nostrils and open mouth like kamikazes. I also felt the occasional tell-tale soft nagging of mosquitoes landing on my arms and legs and knew I may be expending energy during my hike swatting them away. But this was no reason to turn around and drive home. If you have ever camped in Florida, you accept that mosquitoes come with the territory, and you just lather on the repellant and hope for the best. I wasn't going to let the bugs dampen the beginning of my hike.

I suppose that when I read the advice above from Ms. Friend and Mr. Keatley, I hoped the water would be on the low "ankle-deep" end of the depth chart since Florida had been somewhat dry this winter. I should instead have realized that the water flooding these roads comes not from rain that falls in Florida, but from the watershed of the Suwannee River that reaches northern Florida from its headwaters in Georgia. I realized less than one mile into my hike just how accurate the advice I ignored had been. More than one and half miles of the first two miles of my hike ran on a road submerged over at least half its length. Most of these stretches had high, tight banks bordered by thorny vines and palmetto

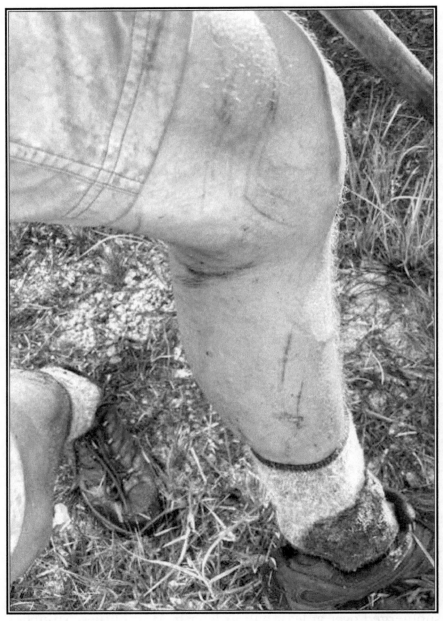

Scratches from thorny vines and palmettos during hike on Florida National Scenic Trail at the Osceola National Forest, April 9, 2024.

and slippery roots, so although I tried to avoid the water by walking beside the road, I slipped in frequently.

I had also overestimated the relief I would receive from the heat by going only a few hours north. It was less than ten degrees cooler in the Osceola National Forest than where I lived, and the lesser clouds also added to the heat. On the bright side, the reduced cloud cover also made it easier for me to see the eclipse just after I made it through the first stretch of submerged trail, and I brought my silly looking cardboard glasses for the occasion. Between the eclipse and the meteor I saw from my tent four days earlier, I was being treated to some special astronomical surprises this hiking season.

Soon after leaving the first submerged road, the Florida Trail entered what would normally have been the most scenic stretch of my hike in, through a relatively dry forest of slash pine. But it, too, had recently been burned, so the scenery was less appealing, the trail was softer and muddier, and the gnats were more intense.

I eventually reached the logging road—the one that was far more submerged with deeper tannic water that would briefly entrap me the next morning—and as the wet sections became longer and less navigable, I began noticing trampled side paths that had been bushwhacked on higher ground beside the trails by north-bound hikers. Mind you, these were not so much trails as gaps between palmettos and those nasty thorny vines. But they were better than nothing and they were not hard to find on the hike in. I also discovered the long boardwalk along the deepest stretch of submerged trail, the only submerged stretch where I noticed a current. It alarmed me when I noticed the boardwalk beside this river washed out so soon that I could not see the dry trail ahead of me, and I was forced to hop down into the muddy stretch of bushwhacked side trail. But I'm sure I was more concerned at that time with getting to camp as quickly as possible to dry my heavy boots and socks and resume life without a 40-pound backpack. This was still only halfway through my 6.5-mile hike in.

Although none of the water obstacles were as severe after I passed the swampy river that would briefly trap me the next morning, they were deeper than those I encountered in the first two miles, so I spent more time becoming too acquainted with slicing palmetto fronds and thorn-covered vines. Even the intersection of the Florida Trail with the road connecting to the campsite was a muddy pond. But I was relieved to finally make it to the campsite.

The West Tower campsite was the first site I camped at during the season that was not a secluded small backcountry campsite, as I noticed when I came within 50 feet of its trailside entrance and heard dogs barking. After rounding the corner, I met two campers escaping the heat in their minivan who let me know that the friendly pooches did not bite. I quickly discovered that this was more of a campground used primarily by parking lot campers rather than backpackers. Located on a paved road, the campsite is free to use and is a collection of relatively secluded parking spots big enough to accommodate RVs with picnic tables and large fire rings filled with cigarette butts. Several campsites had bear-proof steel garbage cans that had more than a little trash near them that the parking lot campers had not seen fit to put into the cans. The only convenience missing from these sites for parking lot campers were electrical hook ups, and several RVs ran noisy generators that could be heard throughout the campground.

Perhaps because of the eclipse, the campground was pretty busy for a Monday evening. Almost all of the first-come-first-serve parking spaces were occupied by RVs, and I suspected I'd spend the night listening to barking dogs, country music, and people drinking beer while throwing cigarettes on campfires. The RVs congregated at the center of the campground in more easily accessible spots, so I was able to find a large campsite on the western perimeter of the campground facing nothing but palmetto and pine. I made the most of it and stripped down to my underwear to deter any RVs who might pull up later and demand to share my spot. None ever came, and the few parking lot campers I encountered were as friendly as could be.

As much as I would have liked to sunset hike, I'd had enough of the submerged jeep roads, so I spent the early afternoon and evening setting up camp, cooling off, and trying to dry my boots. Although the muddy boots did a great job of attracting swarms of insects while perched atop my picnic table, they never dried significantly, even after I later hung them by my campfire. The gnats were relentless as the sun began setting and refused to leave me alone. I paced throughout the campground, trying to see if I could avoid them more in open spaces or near certain types of trees. It became clear that the gnats would follow me anywhere I went, at least until a campfire began. I set up my tent behind a live oak bordering the edge of the campground for privacy, then set to the task of preparing my campfire before dinner.

That task was not easy. The large campsite had two improvised fire circles surrounded by broken cinder blocks, but both were full of partially buried Marlboro Light butts and boxes, crushed beer cans, broken beer bottles, and other trash that the last rednecks saw no need to throw into campsite garbage cans. I found a new patch of sand free from plants and roots, and I swept it clear with my fire stick and dug a flat depression several inches deep. I then dragged over broken cinder blocks and built a new fire ring. I scouted the campground for dry firewood and stacked it between the white trash fire ring and my newly constructed ring. I was now ready to start my fire after dinner, and although I was tempted to light my fire immediately to disperse the gnats, I didn't want to waste wood before nightfall.

Dinner ended up being excellent despite the gnats. I had brought a new dinner of sweet pork and rice, and it now competed with chicken coconut curry as my favorite trail dinner. Of course, I had to share several bites with the gnats, who pestered me while I ate and were kept out of my sealable meal pouch only by me zipping it shut between bites. But after a day like that, every bite was better than the last.

The trip began improving significantly after night fell. Because of the height and density of the pines, sunset was a new experience, as the fading beams of sunlight outlined the vertical trunks of the pines like bars of a jailhouse window. The fire was also a god send. I lit it immediately after I finished dinner, not long after the sun dipped below the horizon, and despite the wet conditions on the trail, the low humidity allowed the fire to last for more than three hours. It also dispersed the gnats and mosquitoes, which seemed to go to bed anyway once night fell. I finally had relief from the bugs.

I was also pleasantly surprised by the campground and what I had unnecessarily feared about my neighbors. These campers were not the partying type, but good people who enjoyed the serenity of the outdoors as much as I did. The generators clicked off before dinner and I heard no music and nothing but the distant crackle of burning logs after dusk arrived. My neighbors were also respectful with light, and through the dense fields of pine, I saw virtually no lights from RVs, tents, or vehicles. Though I was not technically in the deep backcountry, I felt like I was even before the moon appeared. It was refreshing to have my always-expect-the-worst negativity put in its place.

But just in case anyone came, I got naked and stayed naked long after my camp shower. I knew this was my last trip of the season, and walking around a campfire naked was perhaps the most childish and immature discovery I made while solo backpacking, and I'm a very immature 47-year-old. After a day of persistent torment from gnats, I thought that my twig and berries had as much right to enjoy the freedom from buzzing harassment as the other parts of my body. The nudity also helped keep me cool before I finally retired to the tent at midnight. I still managed to keep any insects from joining me in my sleeping chamber, and I had another sound night of sleep under the stars and live oak boughs one more time.

The sunrise and serenading from the owls returned after I woke up early, and I savored every last second that I could from my tent. I gazed at the live oak bough above my head like a sweetheart wishing her betrothed goodbye as he left for war. The worst mosquitoes I encountered during the entire trip greeted me as I exited my tent and welcomed them with my urine dump, but it was still cool enough to pull the sleeves of my long-sleeve shirt down and its hood over my head. We all had M&M oatmeal and jet fuel coffee together while watching sun beams pierce the pines like light through the teeth of a comb that I did not have to brush my matted hair. I did not linger as I had at the Green Swamp, and I tried to convince myself that the water on the trails would have dried a bit while I slept.

But at least I knew what I was in for, and my boots were already wet. What I hadn't appreciated was how much harder it would be to find the exits to the bushwhacked bypass lanes hacked previously by north-bound thru hikers when I returned on the trail in the opposite direction. I chose incorrectly more often, and even before I got myself lost in the cold cypress swamp near the washed-out boardwalk, I paid the price of incorrect judgment by wrapping my knees in the thorny vines and falling into serrating palmetto fronds repeatedly. Before I even failed to find that washed out boardwalk, my legs and arms were already bleeding, as if overprotective cats had attacked me while I flirted with a lonely librarian.

As I intended to imply at the beginning of this book, the adventure of finding my way through the waist deep cypress swamp was a turning point during the hike, after which my typically negative mind switched from distressed negativity to happy pride in my accomplishments. It was fun on a quickly warming morning to be soaked head-to-toe in cool, fresh water, even if almost everything I carried was soaked. The soaking helpfully inspired a change in attitude. Now, instead of looking for often invisible side paths, I walked straight through most of the remaining stretches of submerged trail. Most of them. I stopped making exceptions after the scariest moment of the trip.

Before a particularly long stretch of submerged trail, I decided to detour through a clearly visible bushwhacked emergency lane that ran parallel to the waterway, beginning right after a log along the side of the trail. But right after I mounted the log with my left foot and strode forward with my right, I saw a large, curled form on the ground below as thick and muscular as the arm of a teenage weightlifter. It had dark hourglass splotches atop a bed of orange-gray, and it was less than a leg-length below where I was about to place my right foot. I recoiled in fear and literally jumped back onto the trail, like a white guy auditioning as an extra for a C+C Music Factory video.

I had not studied up on Florida's poisonous snakes before beginning my backpacking odyssey, but I was certain that I had almost ended my trip by stepping on a copperhead, and I confirmed the species on Wikipedia after returning home. I was no longer adequately cooled by the pond water, and my heart raced, wondering how long it would have taken paramedics to reach me had the viper sunk its fangs into my leg.

I now had a decision to make. I could attempt to find a new path around the black water that I could not see through. Or I could walk through the water, hope it wasn't very deep, and hope that copperheads are poor swimmers. The split seconds of hesitation were consumed by a desire to immediately put distance between me and the legless predator, so I sprinted through the water at top speed that was slowed to a steady speedwalk once the water rose to my thighs. I never looked back to see if I was being chased, and instead extended a middle finger behind me as I screamed F-words like a foul-mouthed clown being attacked by bees. For the rest of the hike, I ran quickly through every remaining stretch of submerged trail, but mercifully saw no more snakes.

But I still became nostalgic in the last two miles before I reached my car. The pines beside the old jeep road were similar to the rest, but Spielberg shot a video anyway to document the end of the adventure for posterity. When I finally spotted my non-vandalized vehicle through the burnt palmettos at the trailhead, I wiped back a tear or two.

But I couldn't let go of the trail just yet. The Osceola Shelter was less than one mile southbound from the Turkey Lake trailhead, and I still had some trail mix left. There was only one place worth enjoying my last trail mix of the backpacking season. I didn't even drop any of my gear and took the entire backpack the half mile southeast down the stretch of the Florida Trail I had chosen incorrectly to bypass.

Here was the piece of Eden I had been hoping to find. Gone were the burned palmettos and pine trunks and flooded trails, and I was again in a pristine forest of pines as thick as pillars at the Parthenon nudging the curves of the grassy trail side-to-side like frozen bumper cars. The gray metallic roof of the Osceola Shelter eventually popped up from the forest floor like the head of a mushroom. I made my way there, stripped off my pack and placed it beside me on the bench of the picnic table, propped my wet boots on my camp stool, and reclined in ecstasy while gobbling the last of my trail mix and water. I chuckled at the adversity I had endured over the last day and wondered if I'd experience it again next season.

I was still not ready to leave Neverland. My sled dogs still wanted to run, but I'd had enough of sloshing through water, and I still had three hours of driving ahead of me. So I crossed the bridge beside the shelter and resolved to continue hiking down the trail until I met ankle deep water, then I'd turn around and return to my car and head home once and for all.

The water arrived a half mile past the shelter, and I bid it adieu with one last outdoor restroom break. I turned around, began the hike back, and woke up Spielberg and the douchey DJ for footage. I took several videos of the majestic pine forest as I hiked back to my car as slowly as the sled dogs would allow. (My legs would later cramp so severely during the drive home on I-75 that I almost needed to pull over.)

When I returned to the car, I continued tradition by taking off my shirt, socks, and boots and hanging them from my open car doors. I then sat reclined under my rear door while eating cheese sticks and sliced turkey pepperoni, now donning the Florida Gators trucker hat that had become my yellow jersey after a successful hike. Now smelling as bad as I had ever smelled and wanting to remove dead gnats and spider webs from my hair, I indulged in one last fit of public nudity by stripping off my underwear and drenching my hair in travel shampoo that I allowed to rinse down my sweat-soaked body. I even waved hello at several passing truckers and presumably caused more than one trucker to throw up in his mouth. It was finally time to return to the real world and back to practicing law and coping with depression in what I hoped would be a new, happier life one week later.

CHAPTER TWELVE

Epilogue

June 18, 2024: I had come a long way to avoid Florida's heat on the trail. The hour is 11:00 p.m., but you can hardly tell from the way the Scandinavian midnight sun still illuminates the tranquil Baltic Sea in front of me, roughly an hour after the sun technically dipped below the northwestern horizon. It's not dark at all and will barely be dark enough when I retire to my tent at midnight to require a flashlight. I'm tending a fire from wood thoughtfully stocked by the Swedish National Property Board at Bogesundslandets Nature Reserve, a forested island of hiking and biking trails, campgrounds, and rocky beaches across a one-lane causeway from Vaxholm, a town in Sweden about an hour's ferry ride northeast of Stockholm where my wife and daughter are sleeping in our rental apartment. I'm a backpacker now, so I couldn't pass on the chance to do a one-nighter in the Stockholm Archipelago.

Vaxholm is a popular jumping off point for those looking to hop on and off ferries to tour the hundreds of islands in the Stockholm Archipelago. My wife and daughter and I would later hike several miles each in pristine forests on the islands of Sandhamn and Grinda, enjoying quiet lunches with no one

Firepit at Varmora campsite, at Bogesundslandets Nature Reserve, Sweden, June 18, 2024.

else around on our own private boulders facing the lake-calm brackish Baltic. But tonight, I have a boulder beside the Baltic all to myself, save for several families of ducks and a few pairs of swans that have been feeding at the water's edge below me all evening. I have hiked four miles—three with gear after getting off a bus and hitting the trail for a dreamy hike, first through fern covered forests of pine and oak, then for the last two miles beside a fjord before reaching the Varmora campsite.

Varmora is one of several campsites that have wind shelters facing a firepit, with two wooden benches perfect for sleeping on cold autumn nights shielded from snowy Swedish winds under corrugated metal roofs. Along its western wall is a covered shelf stocked with split logs kept dry for campers to warm themselves while snuggling in their sleeping bags in the wind shelter. But the Varmora campsite also has a much more special fire pit slightly downhill from the wind shelter, atop a boulder that melts down into the Baltic and faces north, where the rays of the midnight sun continue to illuminate the sky as we approach the summer solstice.

Knowing that I would find any opportunity I could to backpack in Sweden, I loaded my tent and backpacking gear into my oversized checked bag that I brought on our annual summer vacation. I chose to not sleep in the wind shelter, although I did rest there for 45 minutes while waiting out a thunderstorm that struck moments after I arrived at camp. I instead set up my tent on a grassy patch between the wind shelter and my fire pit, where I had the unique opportunity at such high latitudes in the summer to face northward toward both the sunset *and* the sunrise. As usual, I had a backpacking

Tent at Varmora campsite, at Bogesundslandets Nature Reserve, Sweden, June 18, 2024.

failure. I forgot my camp shoes, then chose imprudently to day-hike another mile through the grassy backwoods east of my campsite after the thunderstorm. The wet grass soaked my boots and socks, so I had to wear the wet boots *sans socks* for the rest of the night and then tiptoe to my tent barefoot over the cold, stony ground. But everything else was a dream come true, a once-in-a-lifetime opportunity.

The fragrant dry pine logs burned long and easily as I spent hours gazing at a sky drenched in slowly darkening brilliant orange and blue. I had no problem lighting the fire just 15 minutes after a surprise shower provided my campsite a second rinsing just as I was finishing dinner around 8:30. No owls joined me on this trip, but I was instead entertained the entire night by rival gangs of ducks competing for morsels from the bladder kelp just beneath the water's surface near the stony shoreline. Pairs of swans also dropped by every half hour or so and were nice enough to even swim in front of the foot of a rainbow that appeared shortly after the 8:30 shower. So as usual, Spielberg joined us for some obligatory trail footage for *My Secret World*; the douchey DJ took the evening off. My family and I had kayaked on this fjord two days earlier and sailed near it a day later. But nothing was so special as sleeping beneath the several-hundred-year-old pines beside the Baltic. I didn't have my live oaks, but I was hardly disappointed. My tent had taken me to some pretty special places since I tested it in my backyard six months earlier.

Before first thru hike at the Green Swamp, West Tract, June 2, 2024.

So my backpacking season technically did not end in the Osceola National Forest less than a week before I returned to work in mid-April of 2024. In fact, I took four more one-nighters in the ensuing two months, including my first thru hike in the first week of June, when I trekked 18 miles through the remaining stretch of Florida Trail in the West Tract of the Green Swamp, starting near the point on the crushed stone road where I figured out how to get back on the Florida Trail in April.

Although I did not face the challenges there that I overcame during my crucible on the flooded trails of the Osceola National Forest, the thru hike presented its own challenges. I had to spend most of the first eight miles of my twelve-mile hike out hacking through barely visible spiderwebs that crossed the trail at face height, each of which had at least one big spider, some as large as baseballs. Even with the four liters of water I brought, I barely made it out with enough water and was cramped so badly during the drive home that I needed my wife's help getting out of my car. But completing my first thru hike so soon was an unexpected and gratifying thrill.

I also continue to hike extensively. I returned to the stretches of the Florida Trail in the east and west tracts of the Green Swamp and the Richloam Tract of the Withlacochee State Forest and documented the terrain and campsites for future adventures. I even reveled at getting my first tick while hiking at Richloam and burning it with the flame-heated tip of my pocketknife blade, inducing it to release the grip of its jaws before I flicked it into a zip lock bag for examination and preservation. I have also been back to Tiger Creek

Withlacoochee River, near the Foster Bridge campsite at the Green Swamp, West Tract, June 2, 2024.

End of first thru hike, at South Loop of the Richloam Tract of Withlacoochee State Forest, June 3, 2024.

Preserve more than once, and of course *LL*, where I return anytime something important happens in my recovery from depression.

I also returned to sailing, gaining more experience by volunteer-crewing 23-foot sailboats during Wednesday night races on Lake Monroe near Sanford. My wife even acquired a paddle board, which I've used at Central Florida's springs now that hiking has been made difficult by the summer heat, cooling myself in 72-degree spring water when the high temperatures and humidity become hard to bear. Throughout the spring and summer, I've enjoyed fires in my Solo Stove at home while staring at the stars as often as I can when I'm not prevented by Florida's summer storms.

My first backpacking season will therefore not be my last. Indeed, I dream of little other than returning to the trail again.

I've also had a pleasant surprise in the months since escaping the Osceola National Forest in mid-April: The rebirth of my relationship with my sister.

During my drive to the Osceola National Forest in April, my sister finally responded to my Yom Kippur email by answering difficult questions about my wedding gift and unnecessarily apologizing and telling me in heartfelt terms that she hoped we could one day be close again. I responded by telling her (accurately and honestly) that although I doubt it would have been in her best interest to be close with me in the past, I think I can finally be a good brother to her now, given my new outlook on life following my latest battles with depression. I also pledged to be more sensitive to her feelings and to actually ask her about her life, rather than have our relationship continue to revolve around only me.

In the months since, I've come to know a wonderful woman that I wish I had not wasted so many years ignoring. I think we've both healed a great deal, particularly by sharing the experiences of our childhood, including those described in my first much more brutal draft of the second chapter of this book. Despite acknowledging the accuracy of my memories of how poorly I treated her when we were kids, my sister has made me feel appreciated in ways I've never felt by anyone other than my wife and daughter. We now talk several hours a week on the phone, and I look forward to each call more than the last. Just as I never thought I'd have a family who loved me for who I am, I never thought I'd have a relationship of substance with any member of the family I grew up with. My sister seems to be filling the void left by the intolerance of my parents. I really, really love my kid sister. I look forward to growing old with her almost as much as I do with my wife and daughter.

I've also begun reconnecting with other friends, including the out-of-state friend from the University of Florida with whom I nearly ended my relationship following his harmless comment in December about not drinking. He's even shared long emails with me about his own vacations and hiking adventures and his sentiments on his own cherished moments with his family as his daughter approaches the end of her childhood. I've still been reluctant to return to my friendships with other friends, particularly given their political leanings and the heated political climate accompanying the approaching presidential election. But I'm hopeful that time will heal any wounds I inflicted or suffered, whether they are real or imagined.

Perhaps predictably, life hasn't been all live oaks and sunsets since I made it out of the Osceola National Forest in April. Although I returned to work as scheduled on April 15th, I had a bit of a rocky start. I came down with Covid the day I returned, which caused me to miss a day and a half of work that first week. I also struggled with further panic attacks that forced me to take off a day or two more of work, including one particularly severe attack that led me to escape on a Friday afternoon to Lake Kissimmee State Park for my first post-return-to-work one-nighter, during which I had an unscheduled emergency call with my therapist from the trail. The problems with clients had not been addressed while I was away, and I struggled to find a healthy way to deal with those issues. I began at times to fantasize about a career after law, perhaps teaching or researching or doing something that did not require working with clients unwilling to listen to advice.

Within a month of returning to work, I felt myself beginning to turn a corner. I finally started sleeping more than four hours a night and miraculously began waking up tired—I never thought I'd be so happy to wake up tired. I was managing new cases, winning hearings, taking and defending depositions, and even feeling appreciated occasionally by clients I helped prepare for depositions. I felt comfortable communicating candidly with my assistant each morning about my mental state, to let her know of any problems I anticipated.

But ultimately, it did not work out with my job at the small firm, as my boss and I could never find a way to deal with the client-related problems that had triggered my need for a sabbatical in the first place. In retrospect, I can now see that these problems would likely have made the firm unsustainable for me even if I had not had the crippling problems with depression and anxiety. Perhaps my depression and anxiety brought an early end to an unsuitable job that spared me from more painful hard times. But when my time with the firm ended, it came as a shock and almost nullified the progress I'd made in my recovery from depression. I had to have several unscheduled appointments with my therapist, and my wife and I even considered checking me into a mental health treatment center in the Appalachians where I could hike while recovering. We ultimately decided that it was unnecessary during a telephone interview with the facility.

But the cliché that everything happens for a reason is not without foundation. Not long after my time with the small firm ended, an opportunity arose for me to join a good friend from law school, working remotely at his Fort Lauderdale office doing construction litigation. He and his wife had been longtime friends with my wife and me, and he met his wife while he lived near us in Orlando when we were all starting our careers. He also already knew about my mental health history and was receptive to my need to have flexibility as I continued to recover from my latest battles with depression and intermittent explosive disorder. We agreed that I would start off slowly and work my way back into form as I learn a new area of the law.

This has been a dream opportunity that I would never have considered had my time with the small firm not ended. As I told my sister, this feels like the professional equivalent of reconnecting with a girl I've always wanted to date but never could before because we were always in relationships, but now that we're both available, we're giving it a go because it feels right. Although I still hope to one day teach law and write more, I'm glad to be back enjoying the intellectual challenge of litigation and am content to postpone my dream of teaching.

I have also made significant progress in battling my demons. The pain caused by the end of my time with the small law firm turned out to be only a temporary setback, and even as I struggled to cope with it, I knew that I was in a better place and was better equipped to cope with it than I would have been even a few weeks earlier. I was learning to deal with the explosions and fits of melancholy and slow down their onset by applying tactics taught by my therapist. I started having more weeks without bad days, even before the opportunity to work with my friend from law school arose.

I could not have improved without my wife. In many ways, the weeks after I escaped the Osceola National Forest in mid-April have been harder than the months before, and my wife has stood steadfastly with me through it all. She's become a maestro at guiding me through rough times, now deftly guessing correctly when to soothe me and let me vent and when to suggest that I stop obsessing and focus on the full half of the glass. She has still had to endure occasional panicked conversations where my mind races and cannot be distracted from end-of-the-world negativity. But those conversations are starting to become rare, and we are both getting through them more easily and with less adverse impact on my wife and daughter. My sister has also been a strong support for my wife, as we've attempted to keep her informed of tough times by letting her help my wife through them rather than help me directly.

My recovery has also been aided by writing this book, which I wrote almost entirely in the four weeks between the end of my job at the small firm and our departure to Sweden for our family vacation. The book started out as an article I wrote about my backpacking adventures the day after I returned from the Osceola National Forest. I shared it with a certain author of backpacking books I've named earlier and asked for publication recommendations. When she asked if I had ever considered writing a book instead, my mind caught fire with excitement. I suppose I'd always wanted to write a book and never had anything to write about. Diana Helmuth gave me both something to write about and the encouragement to write it. I cannot adequately describe how healthy an experience it was to write this book. During the four weeks before I left for Sweden, I spent nine or more hours a day writing when I wasn't exercising, then spent dreamy, stargazing evenings relaxing before fires in the Solo

Stove, thinking about what I would write next. I can't thank Ms. Helmuth enough for her assistance and encouragement.

I've also made other significant breakthroughs. It was in the weeks after I returned to work in mid-April that I finally realized how little I had ever told even my closest friends about my horrors with suicidal depression and at the non-dual diagnosis addiction treatment center in 1999. I ended up sending another atonement email to the out-of-state friend from UF shortly after returning to work in April, acknowledging that he had no way of knowing about those horrors or why I was so upset about his comment about not drinking at the get-together in December. All of it has led me to realize that I can no longer be as secretive about my past and my struggles with depression and anxiety. Although I had justified my secrecy in the first 22 years after my suicide attempt by a need to safeguard my career, I've come to appreciate that my secrecy has caused me far more harm than good. Sharing my struggles with a broader spectrum of friends has liberated me and helped me heal.

I know my mental health is fragile and will require attention and vigilance for the rest of my life. I plan to continue therapy and medication indefinitely, even if the problems that upended my life beginning in December 2023 go into hibernation. The stakes are high, as my daughter and wife are also riding the rollercoaster I've been on the last six months, and we're all ready to get off for a while. I pay constant attention to my moods, avoiding not just extreme despair, but also extreme moments of joy that could easily trigger a new explosion or bout of melancholy. I'm getting

265

better at it, but I know things can change without warning, and I plan to do all I can to be ready when they do.

One thing that has not changed is my relationship with my parents. They still know nothing about this book or my backpacking adventures, nor do I intend to tell them. I did reach out to my mother shortly before I returned to work in April to let her know about my recent mental health struggles and to warn her that I need to keep my distance from her for a while to recover. I also hinted that if she could somehow avoid being so negative with me, particularly about the things I love, there might be room for improvement of our relationship. But I'm not holding out much hope for anything to change.

I have at least found some comfort in accepting the past for what it is and attempting to move on. I can't expect my parents to change. Hardly anyone changes so late in life, and I've only changed because I've needed to do so to survive. I do wonder occasionally if I'll one day regret not having made more effort to reconcile with my parents after they die. But I doubt it. I've seen and heard too much over the years and in recent times to think that my parents are the least bit receptive to my need to be accepted for who I am, rather than who they think I am or want me to be. They're just a bit too set in their ways, like many people of their generation, and they are bombarded with too many messages on television that reinforce their belief that the rest of us are what is wrong with the world. If they ever read this book, I expect them to dismiss the things I've said as cheap shot lies intended only to wound them and deny my own shortcomings.

It is what it is. At the end of the day, I have my wife and daughter, and now also my sister, and that is enough. Writing this book and particularly reading Dr. Aron's book about highly sensitive people has helped me to cope with the difficult realities of my past. For the first time in my life, I'm finally comfortable with who I am and why I am the way I am. Although I could never pretend that the bad experiences with my family never occurred or do not matter, I can now more comfortably live with why they've impacted me the way they have. I'm in a better place, even without my parents.

And of course, I still have my unquiet mind and my passion for travel and adventure. But now I have the added bonus of greater mental stability to help me enjoy them more. This stability no doubt proved indispensable when we had to run through the Newark airport to barely make our flight to Sweden after the two-hour delay of our connecting flight from Orlando. Despite far greater stresses during transatlantic vacation travel this year, I made it without the explosions or panic attacks that accompanied prior trips. Weighing 100 pounds less and fitting more comfortably into the sardine can airliner seats with minimal seat pitch surely helped.

The Prozac and therapy also helped when our flight home from Stockholm was cancelled on the tarmac. As the other passengers raged at post-flight ticket counters about rescheduling flights to the United States, my wife and daughter and I decided that the flight home could wait a few days. We all agreed that the best place to return for three more days of vacation was Vaxholm.

And as a result, the once-in-a-lifetime one-nighter at Bogesundslandets Nature Reserve turned out to not be once-in-a-lifetime after all. The second-to-last night before we flew home, I returned to Bogesundslandets for one more one-nighter, except this time I added more challenging hiking by trekking on the Nasseldalsrundan loop deeper in the park, after having hiked several miles earlier in the day with my family on the island of Grinda.

This time I got more of the challenge I had experienced in the Osceola National Forest. The terrain was much hillier, as I raced from mosquito filled marshes up billion-year-old glacier carved metamorphic hills, at times leaping across shallow crevices between boulders to find blazes. Several marshy sections were overgrown with chest high weeds that were presumably covered with ticks I had been warned about, and I struggled again to find the trail. At one point, I had to stop and search for several minutes to find the fading blaze on a boulder showing me the way on. It didn't help that I had decided to start my hike after 5:30 p.m., or that I had more trouble than expected shaking off the surprising potency of the Swedish lagers I had enjoyed at Grinda. It also didn't help that neither of the two campsites on the Nasseldalsrundan loop were suitable, and that I had to return to the Varmora campsite with almost 3 more miles of aggressive twilight hiking, for a total hike in of more than 7½ miles. It was also surprising when I found two Swedish college kids already enjoying the wind shelter there and, for the first time, had to share a primitive campsite with others.

As before, I adapted and once more enjoyed a once-in-a-lifetime opportunity, but this time no anxiety accompanied the challenges. The locals were nice enough to let me share the campsite, and they even let me have the better firepit with the ducks beside the Baltic Sea. As my feet and body ached from the sunny heat of the now-dry trail, I relished the improvised dinner of Swedish ramen noodles and Swedish sausages I bought from Vaxholm's grocery store. I could not read any of the cooking instructions on the package, but I guessed well enough for a nice seaside dinner. I managed my first campfire ever without kiln-dried kindling despite my prediction of failure. Although I decided to spare my Swedish friends from a naked campfire, I did do a brief naked yuppie shower beside the sea while the last fishing boat of the night passed not quite out of view of my sweaty buttocks. What can I say, I've got to be me.

As the smoke and sea breeze dispersed the mosquitoes and my legs twitched, I laid on the bench beside my campfire for hours (again), staring in glory at the never-ending Scandinavian summer sunset and listening to the Swedish pine crackling in my fire and the ducks searching for more midnight snacks. My mind drifted again and again back to the day's adventures, where this time I was the one hopping up and down stony hills like Super Mario, now with 35 pounds strapped to my back that I hardly noticed in my adolescent glee. The bright orange, blue, and pink sky followed me to my tent, and the centuries old pine was there again beside my tent when I woke up at 5 a.m. to a brightly lit sky. I guess I missed my last sunrise from the trail in Sweden by an hour or two. My Swedish brand instant coffee tasted as good as any coffee I had this season, and as I hit the trail for one last hike out, I wondered where backpacking might take me next.

Wherever it may be, I can't wait.

Sunrise at Varmora campsite, at Bogesundslandets Nature Reserve, Sweden, June 26, 2024.

ACKNOWLEDGMENTS

The story of this book begins with Diana Helmuth, author of (among other books) *How to Suffer Outside: A Beginner's Guide to Hiking and Backpacking*. Having been inspired by *How to Suffer Outside*, I sent a fanboy email to her with a copy of my 16-page article that eventually turned into this book, hoping she wouldn't wince at its length and errors and my poor imitation of her writing style. I did not expect a response any more than I would have from Santa Claus. In one of the most empowering acts of kindness I've ever experienced, Diana complimented my writing and suggested I write this book and in so doing, changed my life. I had never before even thought about writing a book. In the months after she lit my creative fuse, Diana also provided generous guidance and encouragement, despite her own considerable professional commitments. If there is a single person responsible for this book coming to life, it's her. And her writing is like good stand-up, like Dana Carvey sketch comedy. She has set the bar high.

I also owe a debt of gratitude to Douglas Wadle, another author who, like me, moonlights as a writer without quitting his day job (he is a physician). Doug also wrote an excellent book, *Einstein's Violin: The Love Affair Between Science, Music, and History's Most Creative Thinkers*,[29] and he provided me great feedback on early drafts of portions of this book and key insights into the publication process and how to find a

271

publisher. He is also a great brother-in-law, and he and my sister-in-law, Kristin, have provided touching support for my writing and my recovery ever since I made the smart decision to ask for it. Doug and Kristin, as well as my wife's other sibling Rob Decker and his wife Jenn, are also my role models in all outdoor endeavors, as they've been hiking and backpacking many decades longer than I have. A highlight of this experience has been finally becoming a Decker like Kristin, Rob, Doug, and Jenn.

I also am grateful to Jeff Schlesinger and the rest of the team at Barringer Publishing for taking a chance on a middle-aged first-time author who likes to write about farts, public nudity, and delusional rage. Jeff and his team have been a dream fit for this first-time author, and Jeff responded quickly and thoughtfully to all my questions and ideas. Their sensitivity to the subject matter and my eccentricities have made this book as good as it can be.

I owe a considerable debt of gratitude to my sister, Kelly Nelson. In addition to providing tireless emotional support, Kelly reviewed early drafts of several chapters and provided love and encouragement, even when the idea of writing a book still seemed a bit crazy to me. I could write a book just about how much I admire you, and you're a great mother, even to your brother. I'm also grateful to David Adelstein for taking a chance hiring me to practice law with him, but then nevertheless allowing me a few extra weeks to finish the book before I began working with him. His interest in the subject matter and support for my family has also made a big difference in the continued improvement of my mental health. Thank you also to Amanda Brock, who was one of our first friends to have genuine interest in my backpacking when I was still having those nightmares and breakthroughs. She, too, is a treasured family friend. Many others would have provided love and support if I'd had the courage to share my illness or my backpacking odyssey with them sooner, and that's the only reason I've omitted mention of them here as well.

I've been incredibly fortunate to have been guided through my latest battles with depression by Dr. Carolina Zuluaga, my therapist, and Dr. David Kohn, my psychiatrist. They are each a credit to their profession, and they have both gone way beyond the call of duty to help me cope with my demons. Dr. Zuluaga and Dr. Kohn and their colleagues save lives every day, often at taxing emotional cost to themselves, and my family and I would be lost without them.

My wife, Kara Rogers, has been a rock and a rock star throughout the creation of this book and the events it recounts. Thank you for letting me write this, including by sharing cringy personal details of some of our darkest hours, and for your patience with my Hemingway craziness while writing. You are my reward for having survived my adolescence, and your steadfast and courageous support will never be taken for granted, nor will your beauty that never ceases to dazzle me. We've been through so much, and I'll save any sentimentalities for a less public forum, as we both know I cringe at Lifetime movies and generic Hallmark platitudes. Let's just leave it at that you make me look forward to every sunrise and every sunset, and I hope we have many decades more of them together.

My last acknowledgment affords me the unique opportunity to jump into a time machine and talk to someone who will presumably be very different when she reads these lines. My daughter, Claire, is almost 13 now, far too young for the subject matter of this book, and if I have my way, she won't read this until she's much older. Thank you, Claire, for being my friend and everything I dreamed you'd be as a woman and a daughter. Your endurance during the hard times described in this book saved me as much as your mother's support. I look forward to seeing your face every morning, and I will miss you when you grow up and become the light of someone else's life. The kindness I see in you every day reminds me of your mother and makes me proud that I took the risk of having a child. Chapter 2 is for you—I wrote it in case I never have the clarity or courage to share my past with you, to help you through future despair that I hope you never experience and to allow you to know why I am the way I am. You're so smart and so strong, and I can't wait to continue growing up with you.

ABOUT THE AUTHOR

Rob Rogers is an attorney from Orlando, Florida. Rob has published extensively on legal subjects, including articles in national publications like the *Communications Lawyer* and the *MLRC Media Law Letter* and on websites including *Law 360*. He has also spoken at national legal conferences and appeared on the *Bloomberg Law* radio program. Rob graduated with honors from Florida State University College of Law in 2003 and with high honors from the University of Florida in 1998. He lives in Winter Garden with his wife, Kara, and their daughter, Claire.

ENDNOTES

[1] *See, e.g.,* David Brill, *Into the Mist: Tales of Death and Disaster, Mishaps and Misdeeds, Misfortune and Mayhem in the Great Smoky Mountains National Park* (Great Smokey Mountains Assoc. 2017), 12-13, 103-10; *see also* Randi Minetor, *Death in Glacier National Park: Stories of Accidents and Foolhardiness in the Crown of the Continent* (Rowman & Littlefield 2026), 149-57.

[2] As much as I wish I had come up with this insightful term, I borrowed it from the title of an important book about depression. *See* Kay Redfield Jamison, *An Unquiet Mind: A Memoir of Moods and Madness* (Knopf 1995). Or as Vanilla Ice would say, I'm *sampling* the term.

[3] Diana Helmuth, *How to Suffer Outside: A Beginner's Guide to Hiking and Backpacking* (Mountaineers Books 2021).

[4] Philip William Gold, M.D., *Breaking Through Depression: A Guide to the Next Generation of Research and Revolutionary New Treatments* (Twelve 2023), 12-13.

[5] Albert C. Hine, *Geologic History of Florida: Major Events That Formed the Sunshine State* (University Press of Fla. 2013), 26-29.

[6] Hine, *Geologic History of Florida,* 26.

[7] Hine, *Geologic History of Florida,* 26, 138.

[8] Hine, *Geologic History of Florida,* 39-41.

[9] Hine, *Geologic History of Florida,* 138-41.

[10] Hine, *Geologic History of Florida,* 145-46.

[11] Hine, *Geologic History of Florida,* 83-85.

[12] Hine, *Geologic History of Florida,* 55-56.

[13] Hine, *Geologic History of Florida,* 166-71.

[14] Jonathan R. Brysn, Thomas M. Scott and Gary H. Means, *Roadside Geology of Florida* (Mountain Press Publishing Co. 2008), 237-42.

[15] P.J. Benshoff, *Myakka* (2d ed. Pineapple Press, Inc. 2008), 1-3.

[16] Benshoff, *Myakka,* 206.

[17] Benshoff, *Myakka,* 1-3.

[18] Sandra Friend and John Keatley, *The Florida Trail Guide* (4th ed. Watula Press 2021).

[19] Elaine N. Aron, *The Highly Sensitive Person: How to Thrive When the World Overwhelms You* (Harmony Books 2016).

[20] Aron, *The Highly Sensitive Person*, 12.

[21] Aron, *The Highly Sensitive Person*, xviii.

[22] Aron, *The Highly Sensitive Person*, xviii-xix.

[23] Aron, *The Highly Sensitive Person*, xix-xxi.

[24] Aron, *The Highly Sensitive Person*, xxi-xxii.

[25] Aron, *The Highly Sensitive Person*, 66-67.

[26] Aron, *The Highly Sensitive Person*, 66.

[27] Aron, *The Highly Sensitive Person*, 66-67.

[28] "Florida Trail, Turkey Creek to Deep Creek," Florida Hikes! (website), accessed July 12, 2024, https://floridahikes.com/florida-trail-turkey-run-to-deep-creek.

[29] Douglas Wadle, *Einstein's Violin: The Love Affair Between Science, Music, and History's Most Creative Thinkers* (Archway Publishing 2022).

Printed in the USA
CPSIA information can be obtained
at www.ICGtesting.com
LVHW050859271124
797754LV00001B/32

9 781954 396777